LUKE SKYWALKER AND THE
TREASURE OF THE DRAGONSNAKES

Designer
David Nestelle

Assistant Editor
Freddye Lins

Editor
Randy Stradley

Publisher
Mike Richardson

special thanks to Elaine Mederer, Jann Moorhead, David Anderman,
Leland Chee, Sue Rostoni, and Carol Roeder at Lucas Licensing

STAR WARS ADVENTURES: LUKE SKYWALKER AND THE TREASURE OF THE DRAGONSNAKES

Published by
Dark Horse Books
A division of Dark Horse Comics, Inc.
10956 SE Main Street
Milwaukie, OR 97222

darkhorse.com
starwars.com

To find a comics shop in your area, call the Comic Shop Locator Service toll-free at 1-888-266-4226

First edition: February 2010
ISBN 978-1-59582-347-2

10 9 8 7 6 5 4 3 2 1
Printed in China

LUKE SKYWALKER AND THE TREASURE OF THE DRAGONSNAKES

Script **Tom Taylor**

Art **Daxiong**

Lettering **Michael Heisler**

Cover art **Daxiong**

Dark Horse Books®

**THIS STORY TAKES PLACE DURING
STAR WARS: THE EMPIRE STRIKES BACK.**

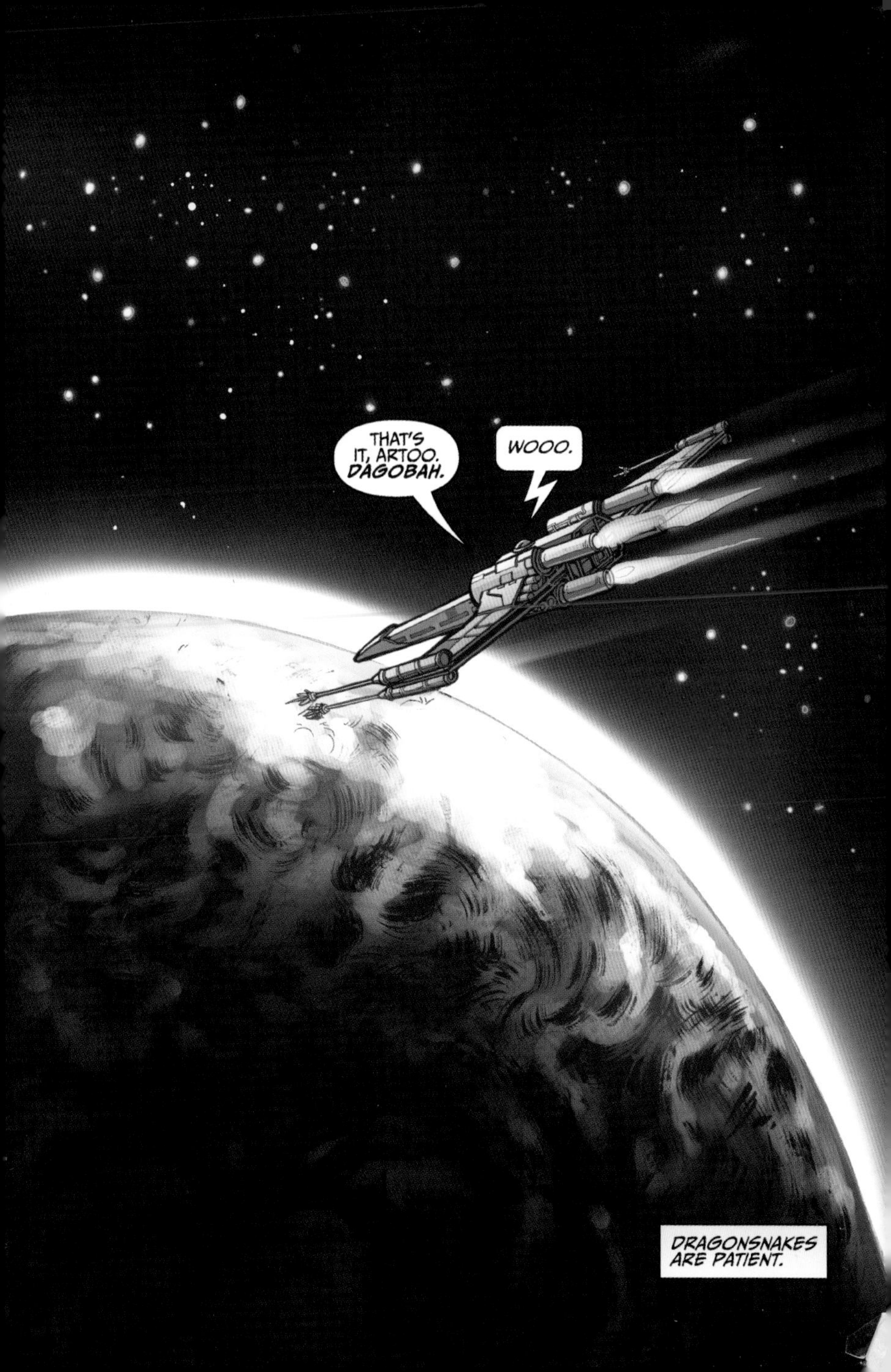
THAT'S IT, ARTOO. DAGOBAH.
WOOO.
DRAGONSNAKES ARE PATIENT.

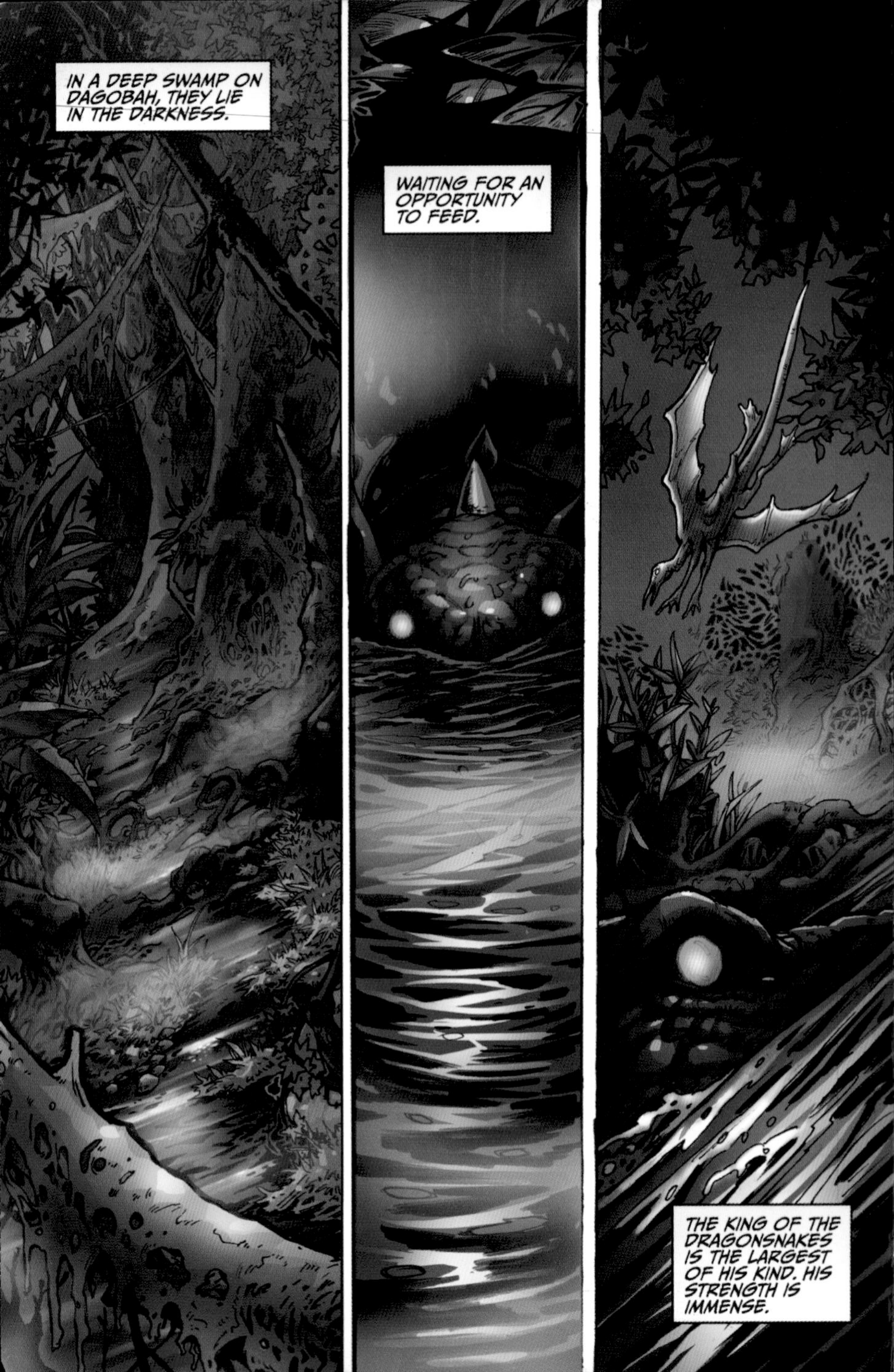
IN A DEEP SWAMP ON DAGOBAH, THEY LIE IN THE DARKNESS.
WAITING FOR AN OPPORTUNITY TO FEED.
THE KING OF THE DRAGONSNAKES IS THE LARGEST OF HIS KIND. HIS STRENGTH IS IMMENSE.

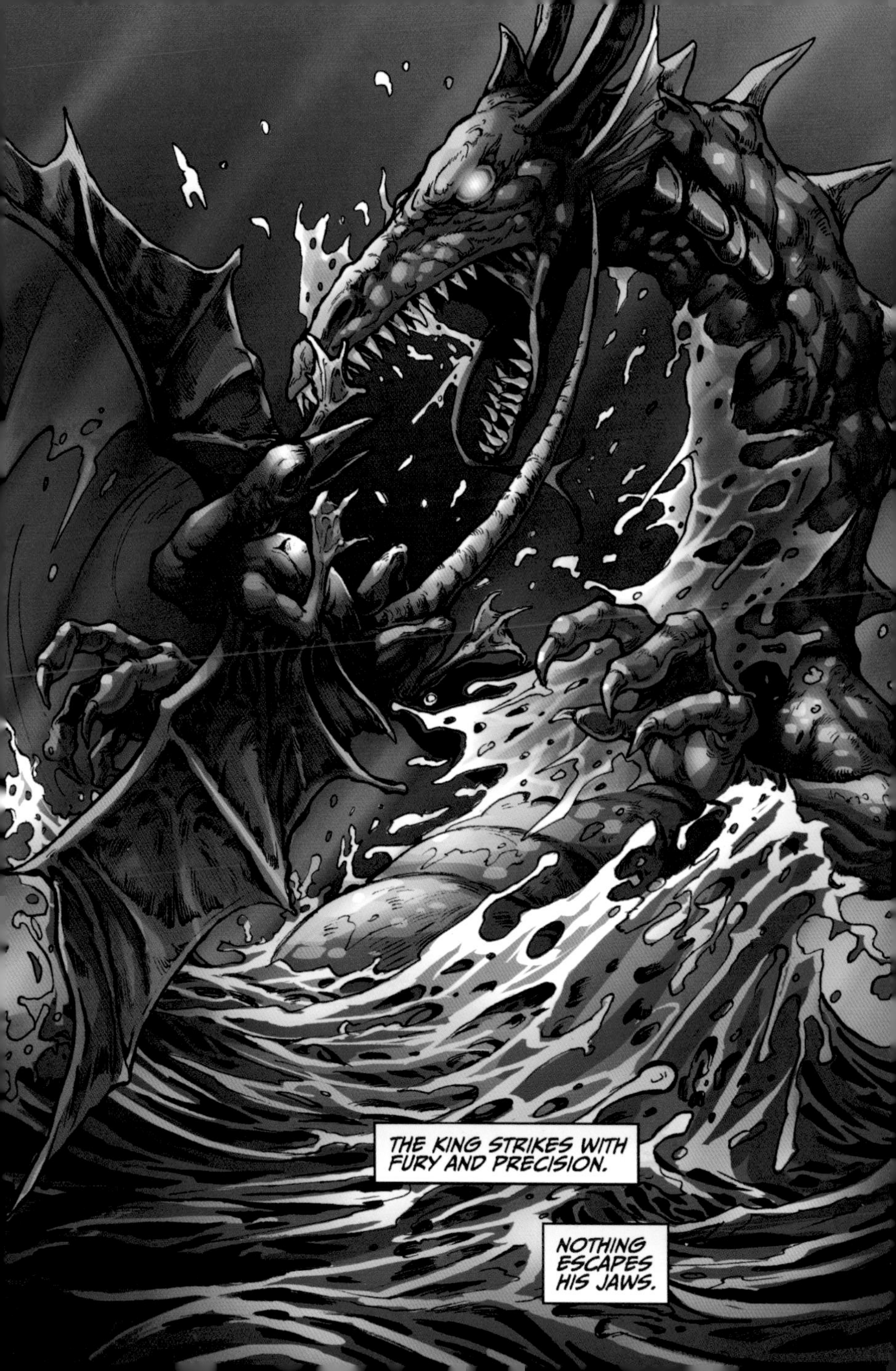
THE KING STRIKES WITH FURY AND PRECISION.
NOTHING ESCAPES HIS JAWS.

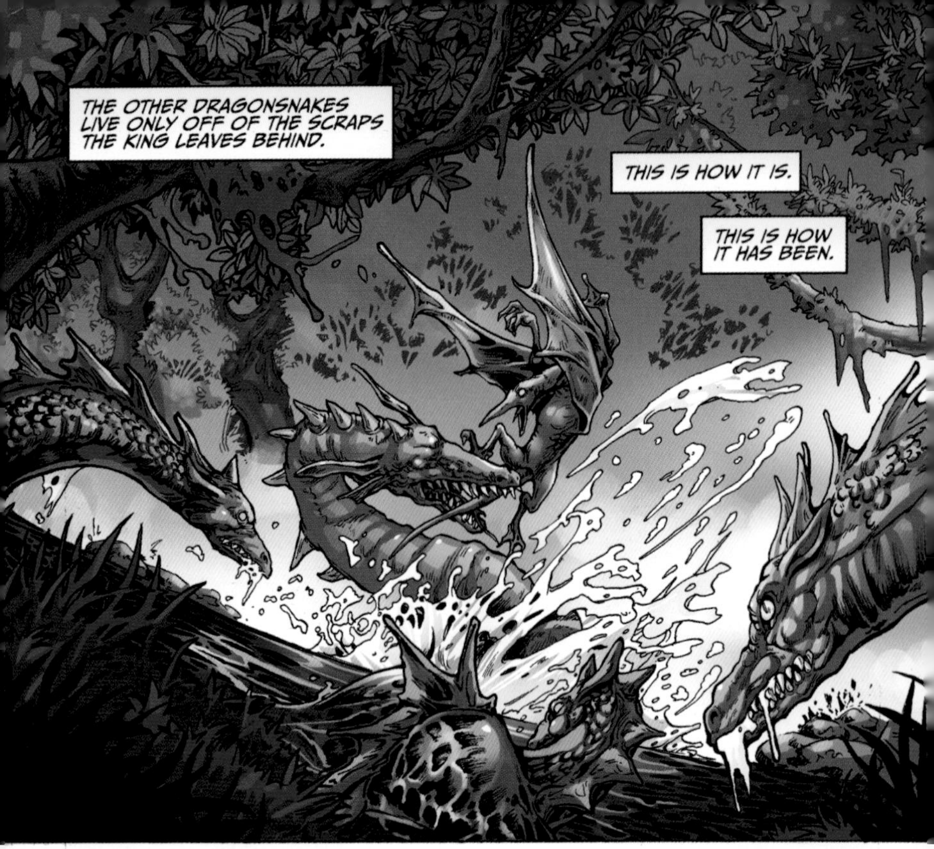
THE OTHER DRAGONSNAKES LIVE ONLY OFF OF THE SCRAPS THE KING LEAVES BEHIND.
THIS IS HOW IT IS.
THIS IS HOW IT HAS BEEN.

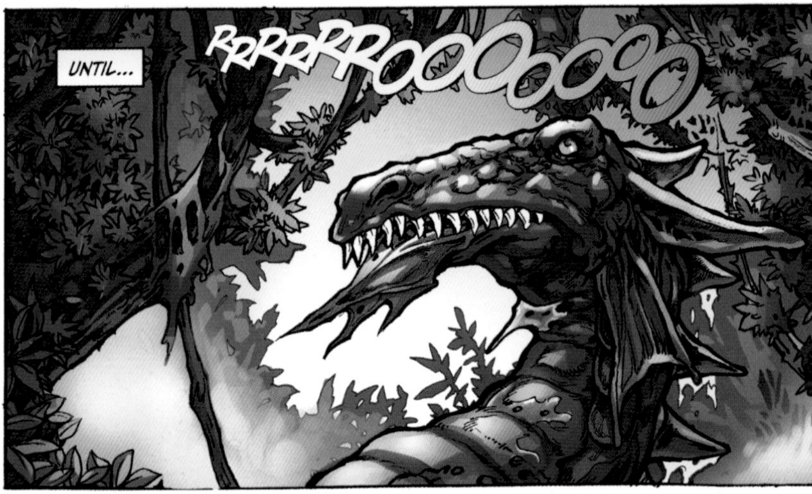
UNTIL...
RRRRRROOOOOOOO

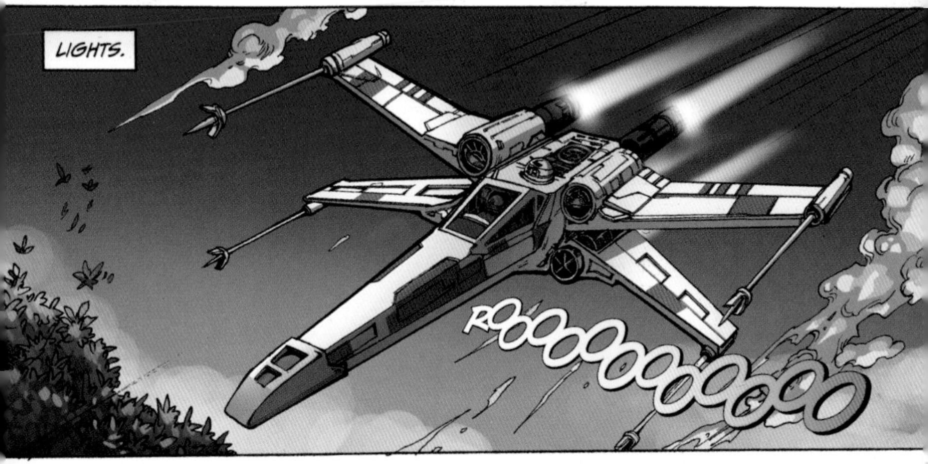
LIGHTS.
ROOOOOOOOOOOO

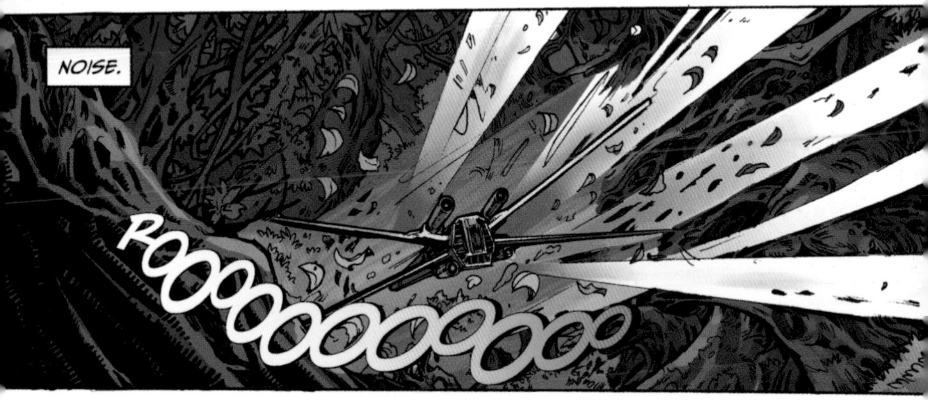
NOISE.
ROOOOOOOOOOOOO

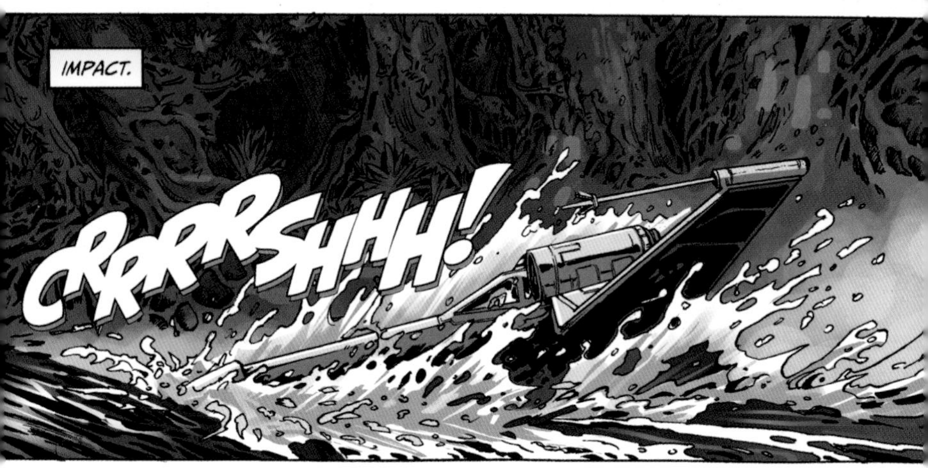
IMPACT.
CRRRSHHH!

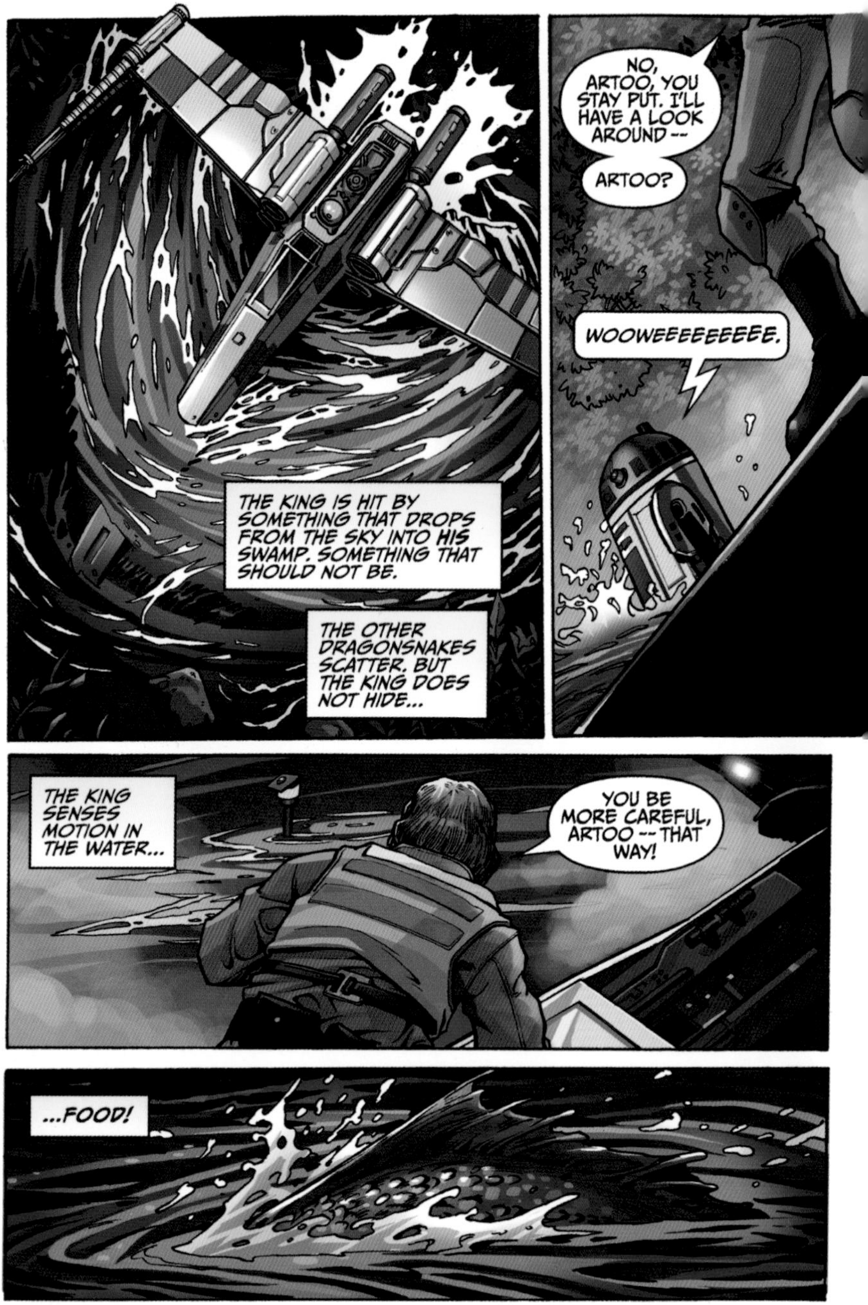
THE KING IS HIT BY SOMETHING THAT DROPS FROM THE SKY INTO HIS SWAMP. SOMETHING THAT SHOULD NOT BE.
THE OTHER DRAGONSNAKES SCATTER. BUT THE KING DOES NOT HIDE...
NO, ARTOO, YOU STAY PUT. I'LL HAVE A LOOK AROUND --
ARTOO?
WOOWEEEEEEEEE.
THE KING SENSES MOTION IN THE WATER...
YOU BE MORE CAREFUL, ARTOO -- THAT WAY!
...FOOD!

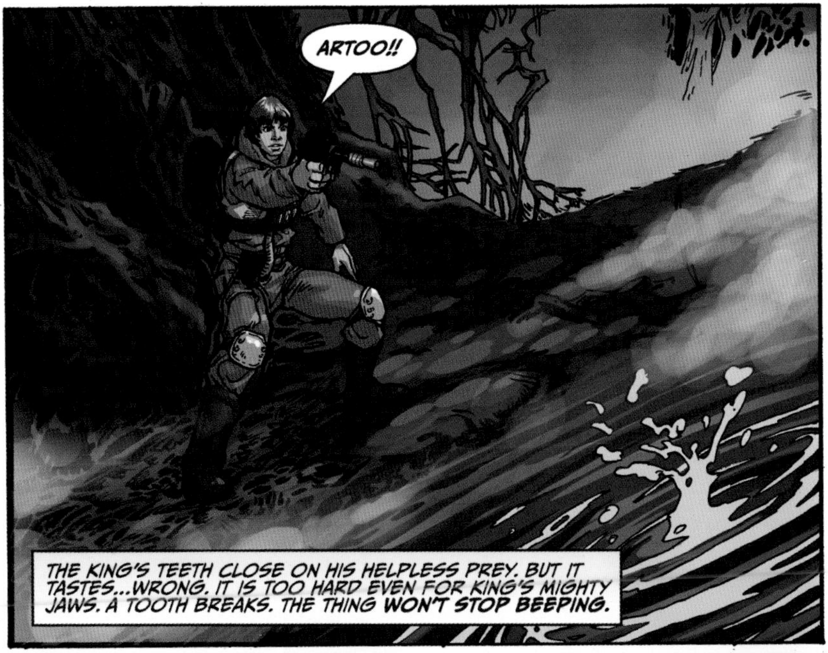
ARTOO!!
THE KING'S TEETH CLOSE ON HIS HELPLESS PREY. BUT IT TASTES...WRONG. IT IS TOO HARD EVEN FOR KING'S MIGHTY JAWS. A TOOTH BREAKS. THE THING WON'T STOP BEEPING.

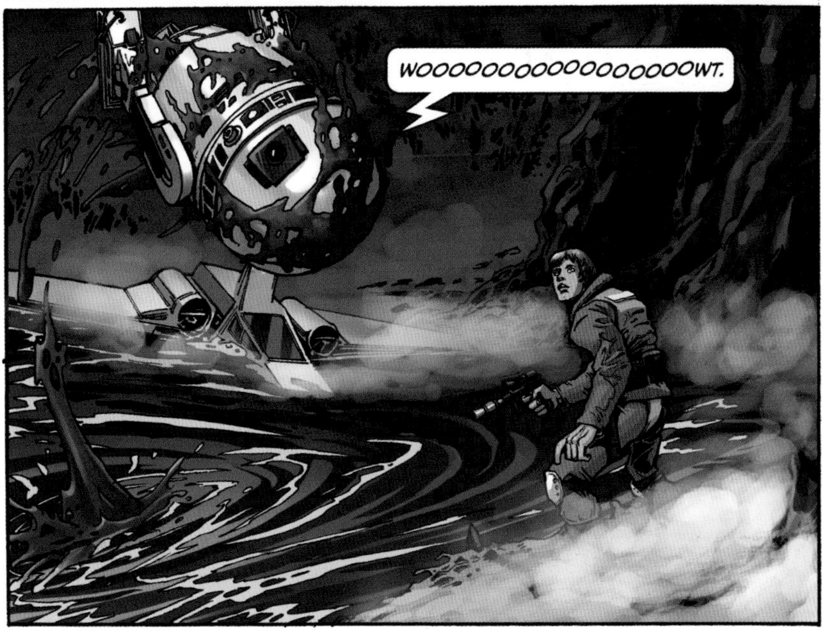
WOOOOOOOOOOOOOOOOOWT.

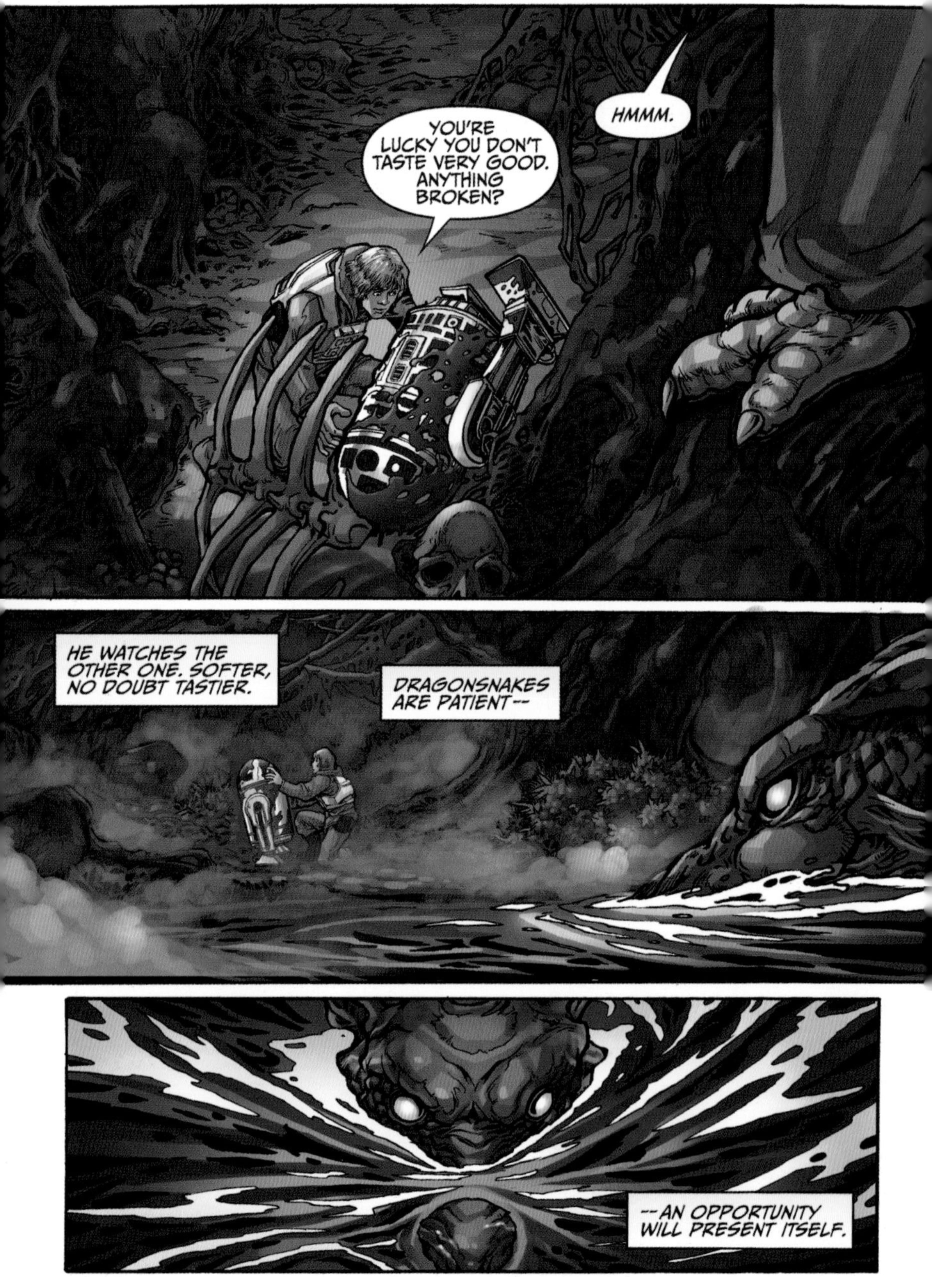
HMMM.
YOU'RE LUCKY YOU DON'T TASTE VERY GOOD. ANYTHING BROKEN?
HE WATCHES THE OTHER ONE. SOFTER, NO DOUBT TASTIER.
DRAGONSNAKES ARE PATIENT--
--AN OPPORTUNITY WILL PRESENT ITSELF.

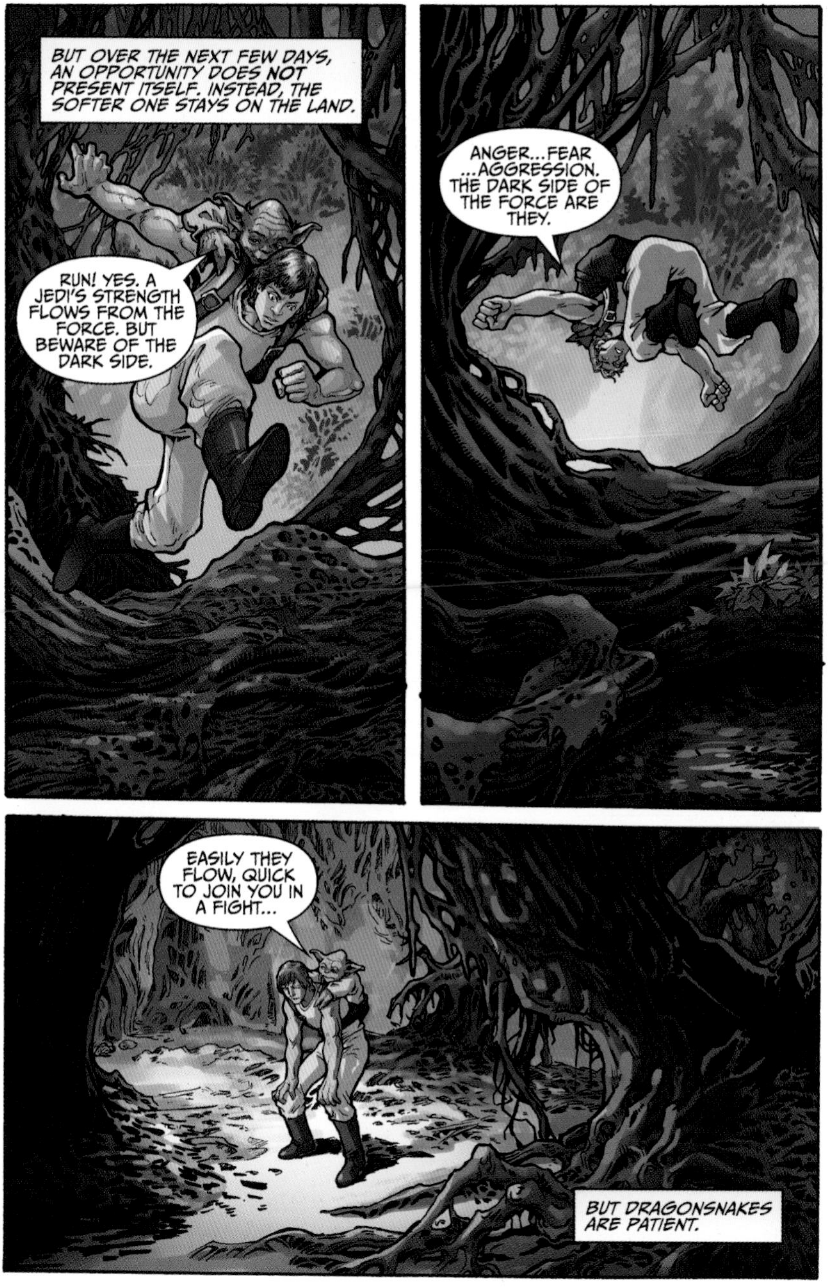
BUT OVER THE NEXT FEW DAYS, AN OPPORTUNITY DOES NOT PRESENT ITSELF. INSTEAD, THE SOFTER ONE STAYS ON THE LAND.
RUN! YES. A JEDI'S STRENGTH FLOWS FROM THE FORCE. BUT BEWARE OF THE DARK SIDE.
ANGER...FEAR ...AGGRESSION. THE DARK SIDE OF THE FORCE ARE THEY.
EASILY THEY FLOW, QUICK TO JOIN YOU IN A FIGHT...
BUT DRAGONSNAKES ARE PATIENT.

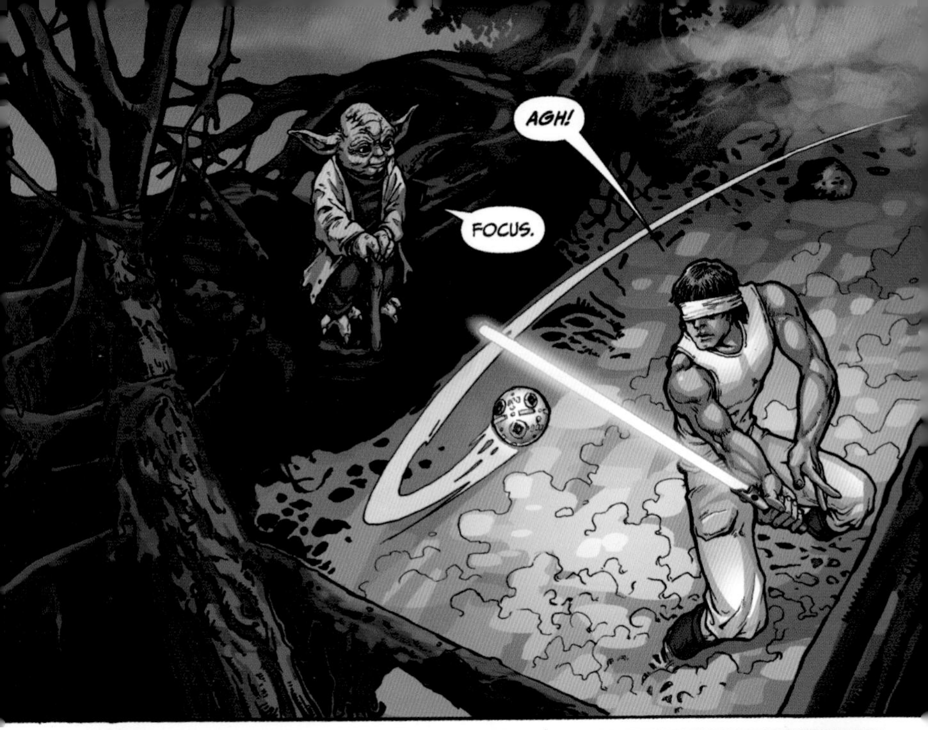
AGH!
FOCUS.

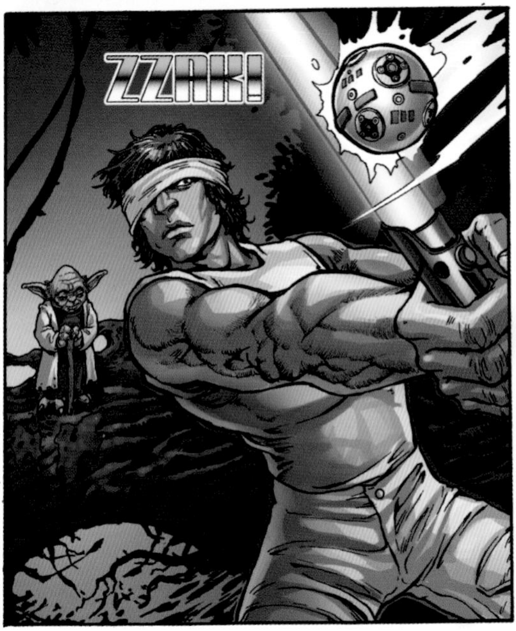
ZZAK!

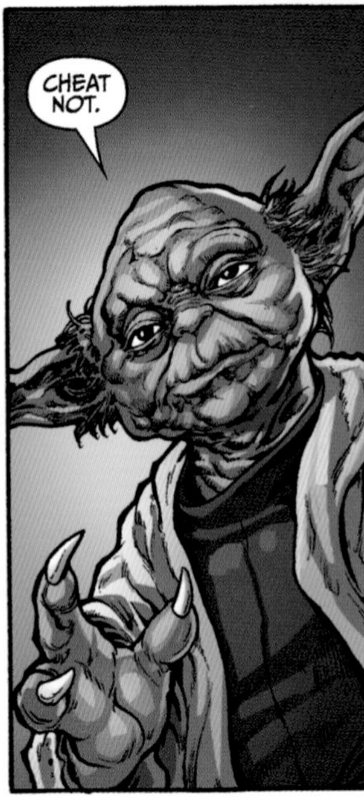
CHEAT NOT.

MASTER YODA?
HMM?
HOW WILL STANDING ON MY HEAD HELP ME LEARN TO USE THE FORCE?
ALWAYS QUESTIONING, YOU ARE. NEVER ACCEPTING. EIGHT HUNDRED YEARS HAVE I TRAINED JEDI. STILL, YOU QUESTION. STILL YOU DOUBT.
I'M SORRY, MASTER YODA.
YOUR MOUTH, CLOSE. YOUR THOUGHTS, STOP. *FEEL* THE FORCE.
WOA...

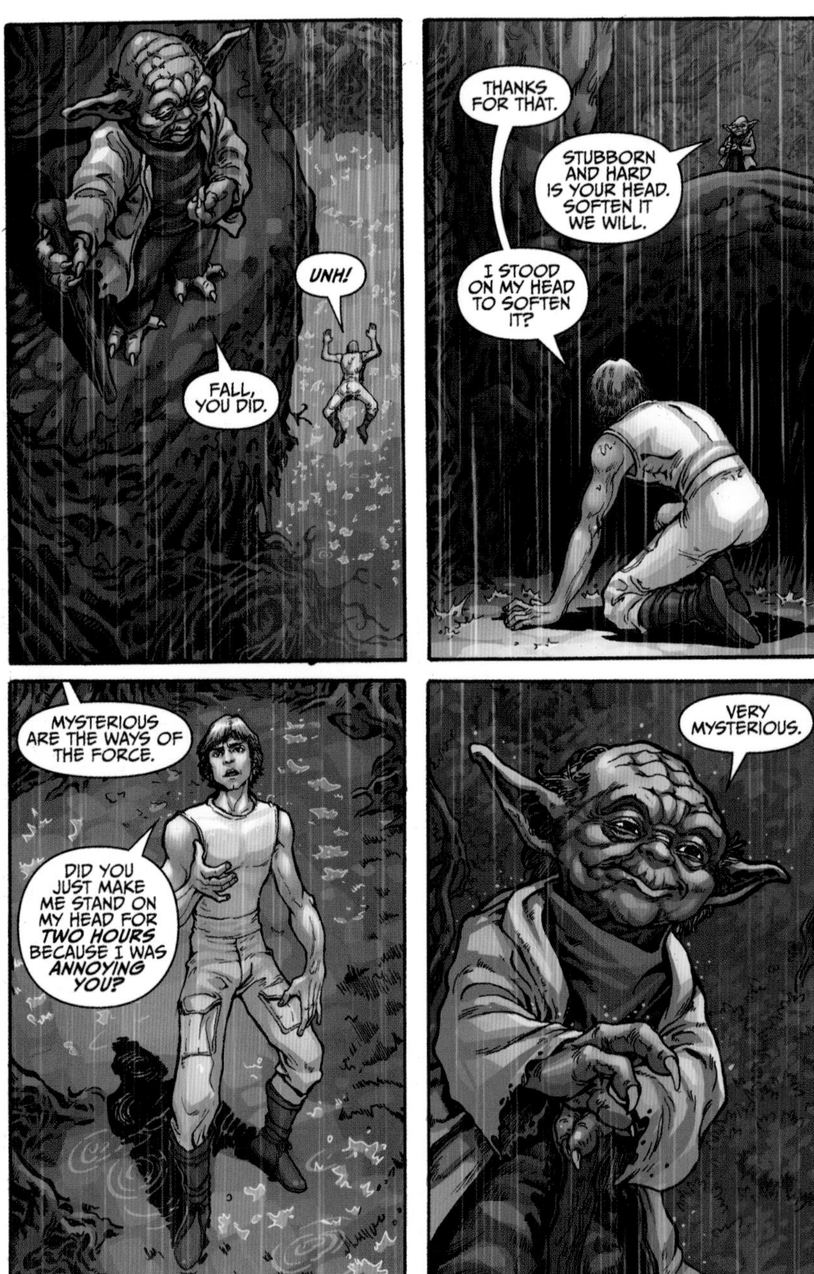
UNH!
FALL, YOU DID.
THANKS FOR THAT.
STUBBORN AND HARD IS YOUR HEAD. SOFTEN IT WE WILL.
I STOOD ON MY HEAD TO SOFTEN IT?
MYSTERIOUS ARE THE WAYS OF THE FORCE.
DID YOU JUST MAKE ME STAND ON MY HEAD FOR TWO HOURS BECAUSE I WAS ANNOYING YOU?
VERY MYSTERIOUS.

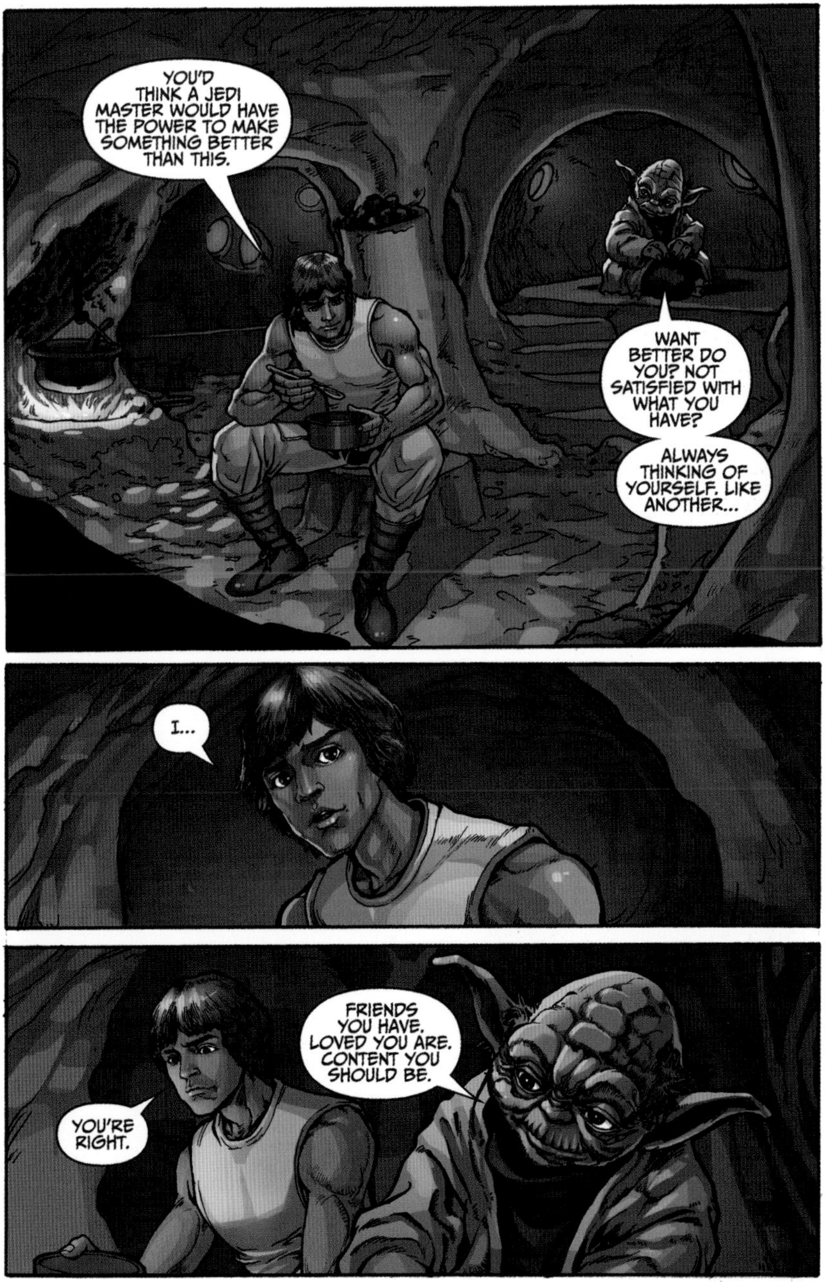
YOU'D THINK A JEDI MASTER WOULD HAVE THE POWER TO MAKE SOMETHING BETTER THAN THIS.
WANT BETTER DO YOU? NOT SATISFIED WITH WHAT YOU HAVE?
ALWAYS THINKING OF YOURSELF. LIKE ANOTHER...
I...
FRIENDS YOU HAVE. LOVED YOU ARE. CONTENT YOU SHOULD BE.
YOU'RE RIGHT.

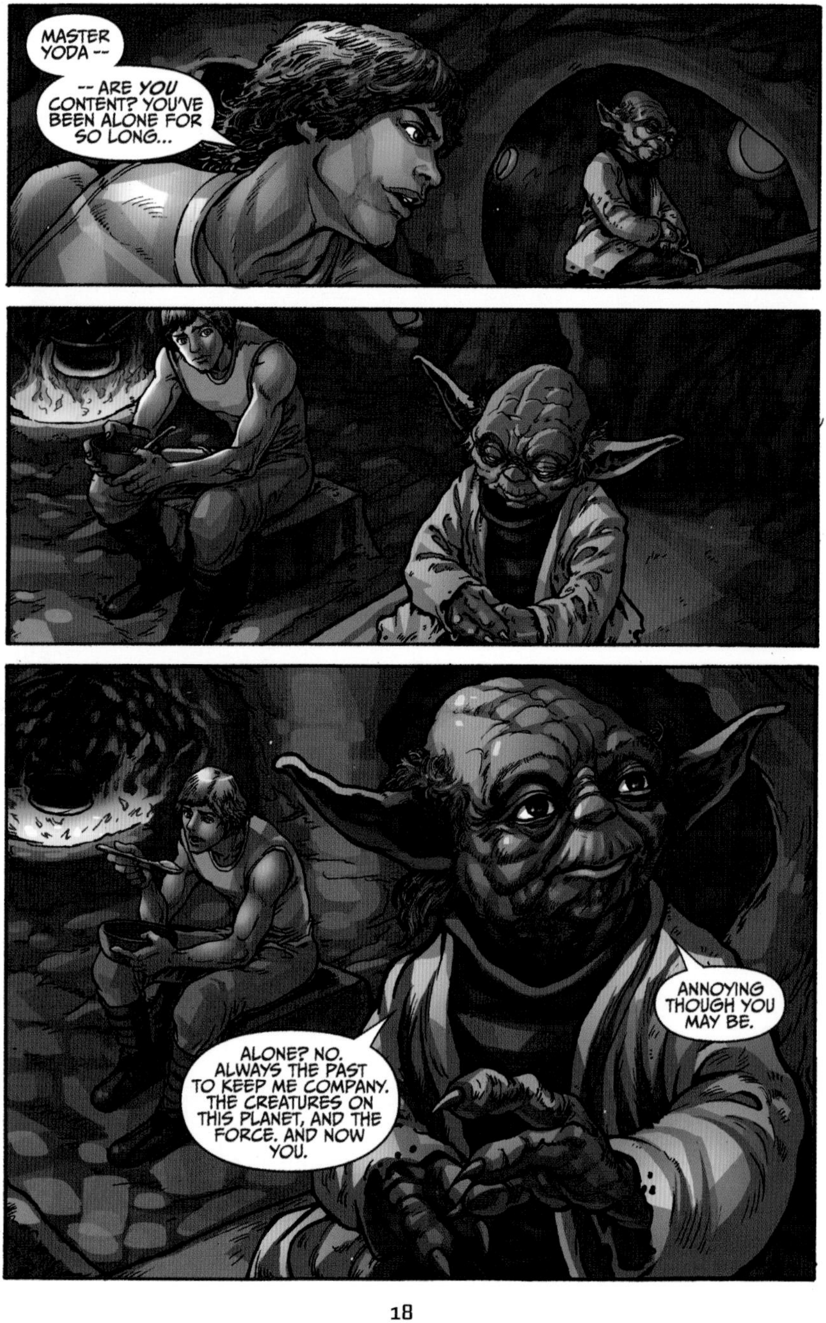
MASTER YODA --
-- ARE YOU CONTENT? YOU'VE BEEN ALONE FOR SO LONG...
ALONE? NO. ALWAYS THE PAST TO KEEP ME COMPANY. THE CREATURES ON THIS PLANET, AND THE FORCE. AND NOW YOU.
ANNOYING THOUGH YOU MAY BE.

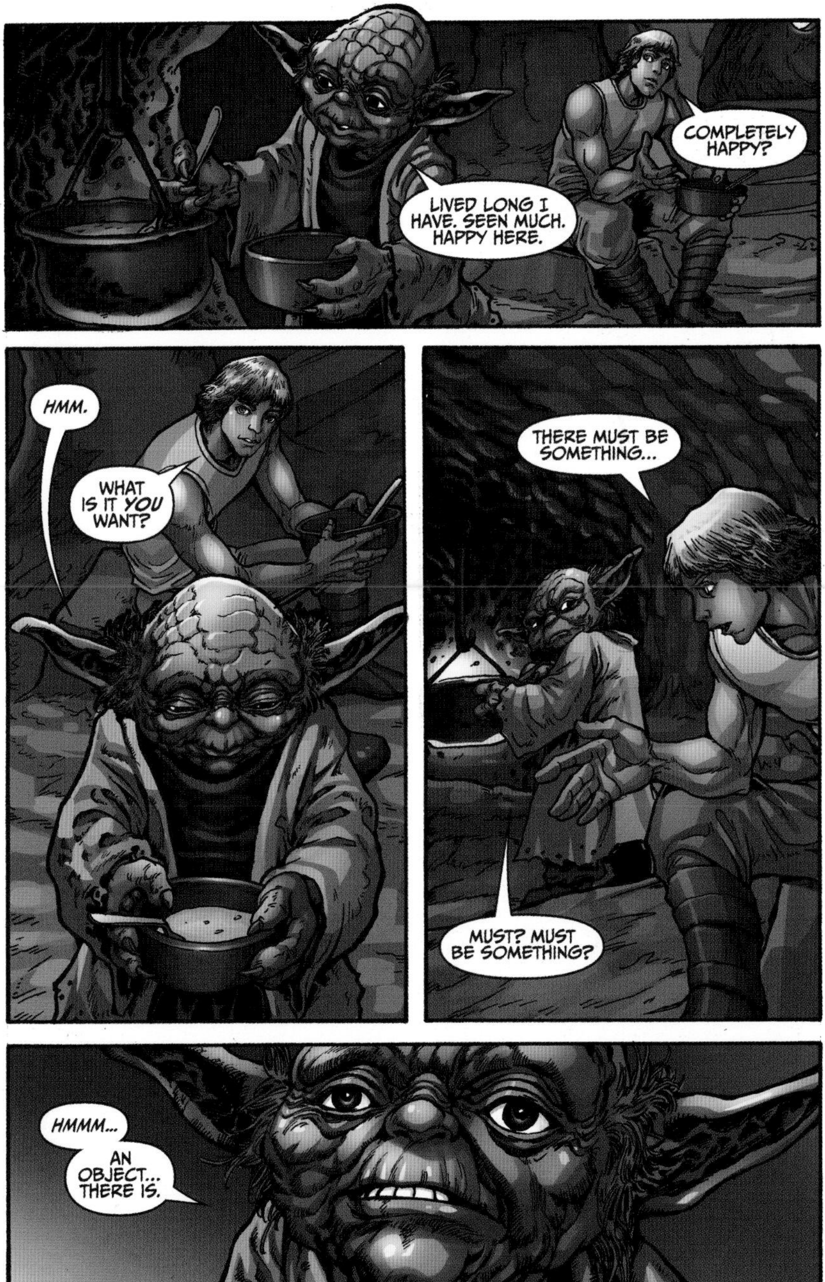
LIVED LONG I HAVE. SEEN MUCH. HAPPY HERE.
COMPLETELY HAPPY?
HMM.
WHAT IS IT *YOU* WANT?
THERE MUST BE SOMETHING...
MUST? MUST BE SOMETHING?
HMMM...
AN OBJECT... THERE IS.

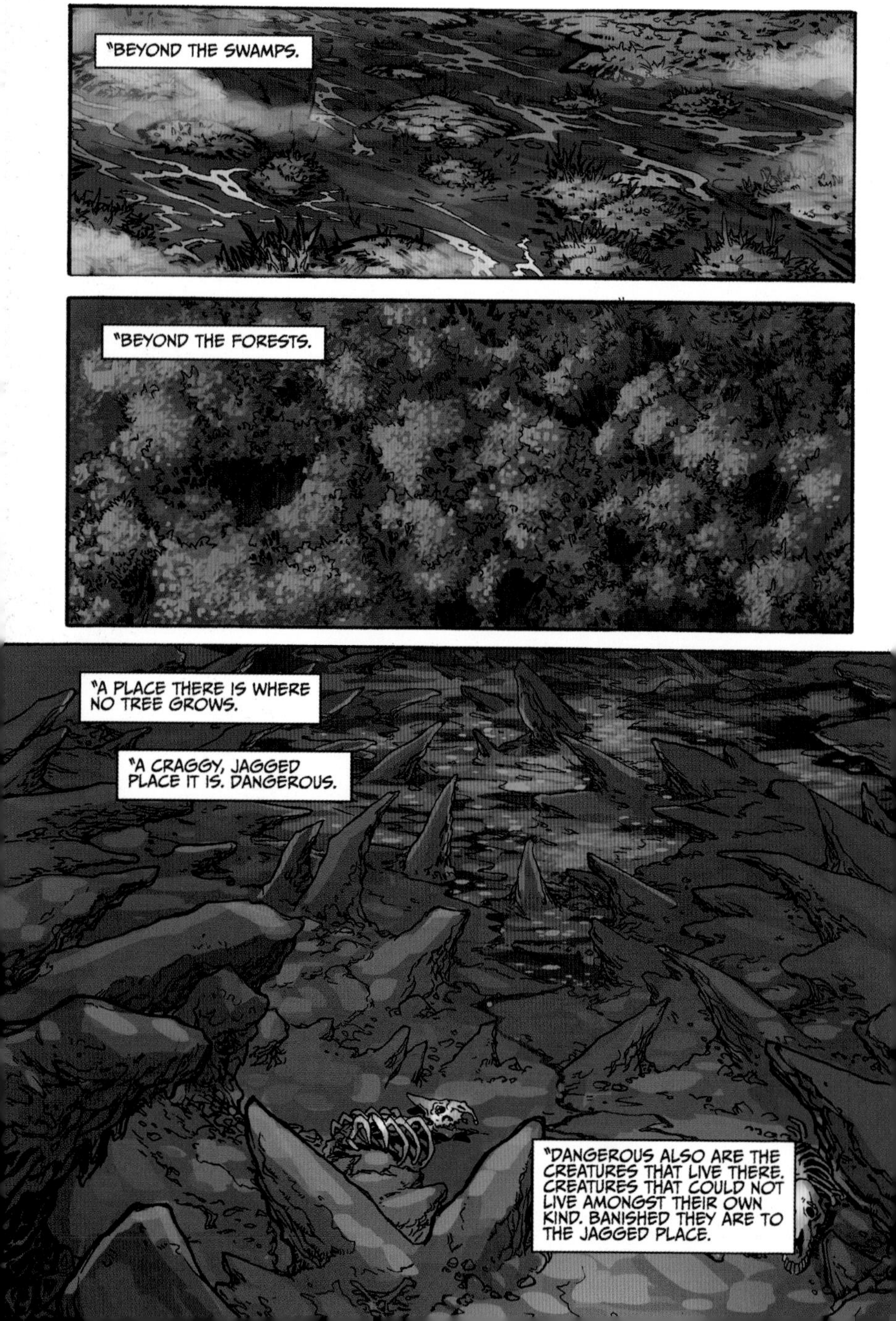
"BEYOND THE SWAMPS.
"BEYOND THE FORESTS.
"A PLACE THERE IS WHERE NO TREE GROWS.
"A CRAGGY, JAGGED PLACE IT IS. DANGEROUS.
"DANGEROUS ALSO ARE THE CREATURES THAT LIVE THERE. CREATURES THAT COULD NOT LIVE AMONGST THEIR OWN KIND. BANISHED THEY ARE TO THE JAGGED PLACE.

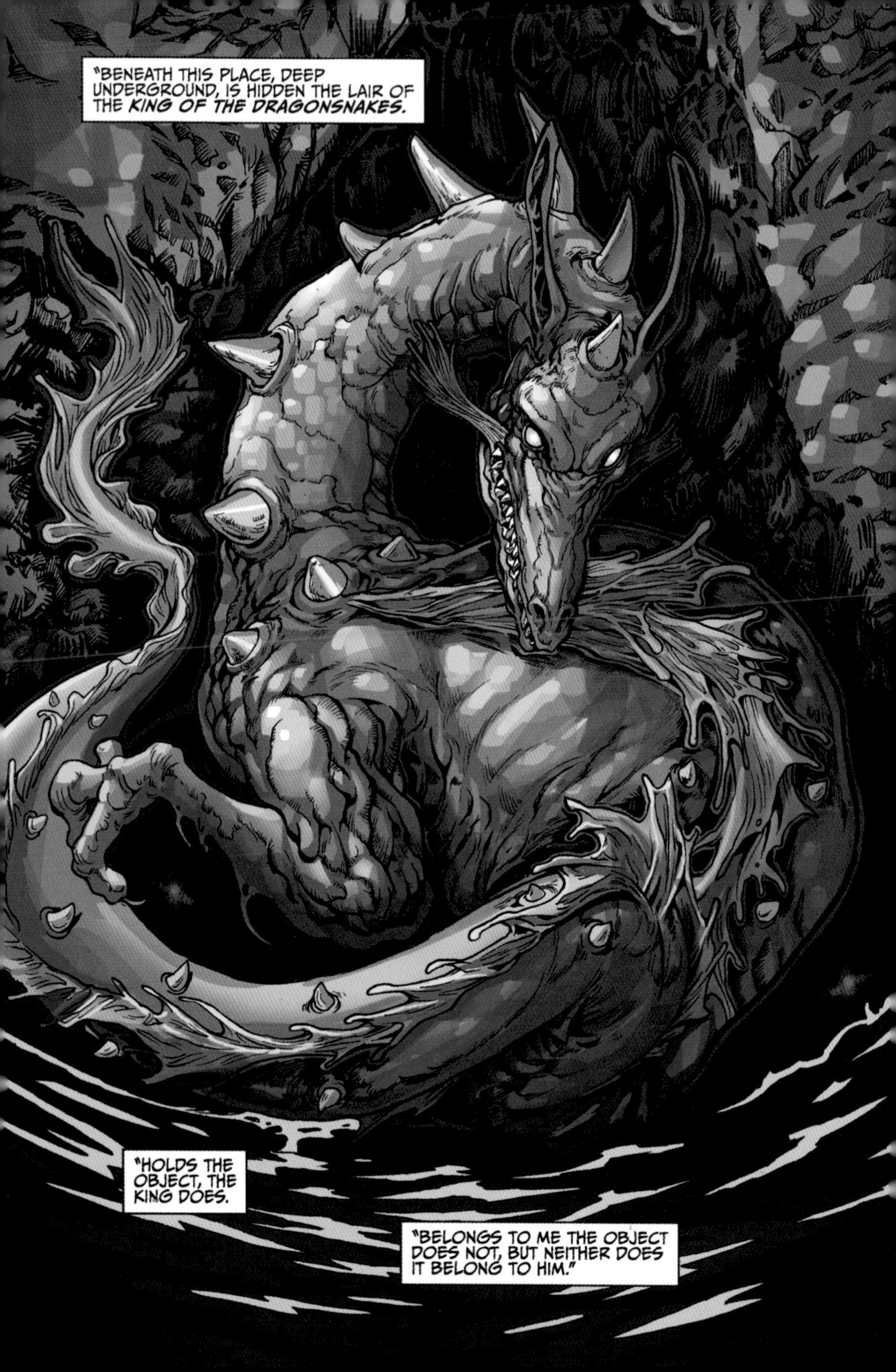
"BENEATH THIS PLACE, DEEP UNDERGROUND, IS HIDDEN THE LAIR OF THE *KING OF THE DRAGONSNAKES.*
"HOLDS THE OBJECT, THE KING DOES.
"BELONGS TO ME THE OBJECT DOES NOT, BUT NEITHER DOES IT BELONG TO HIM."

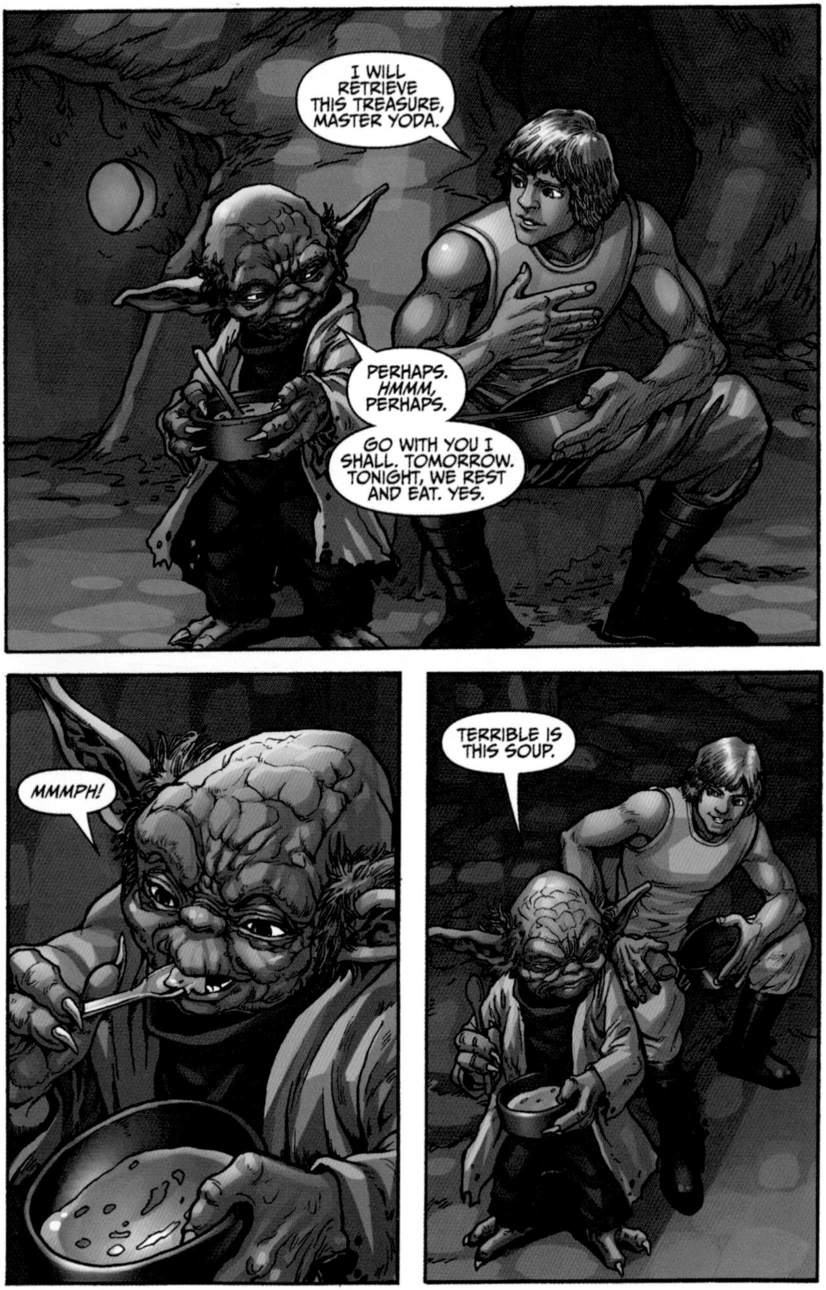
I WILL RETRIEVE THIS TREASURE, MASTER YODA.
PERHAPS. *HMMM,* PERHAPS.
GO WITH YOU I SHALL. TOMORROW. TONIGHT, WE REST AND EAT. YES.
MMMPH!
TERRIBLE IS THIS SOUP.

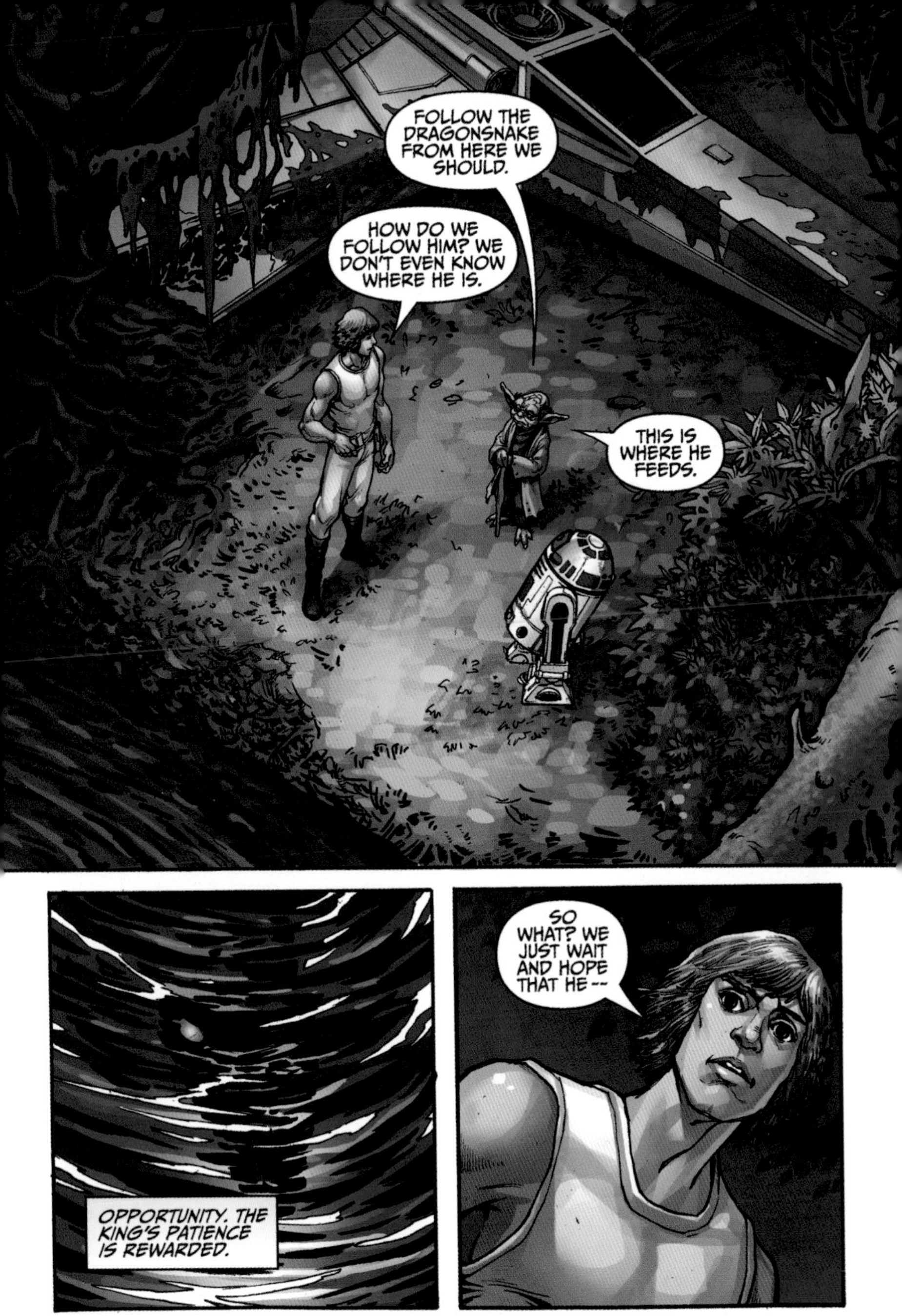
FOLLOW THE DRAGONSNAKE FROM HERE WE SHOULD.
HOW DO WE FOLLOW HIM? WE DON'T EVEN KNOW WHERE HE IS.
THIS IS WHERE HE FEEDS.
OPPORTUNITY. THE KING'S PATIENCE IS REWARDED.
SO WHAT? WE JUST WAIT AND HOPE THAT HE--

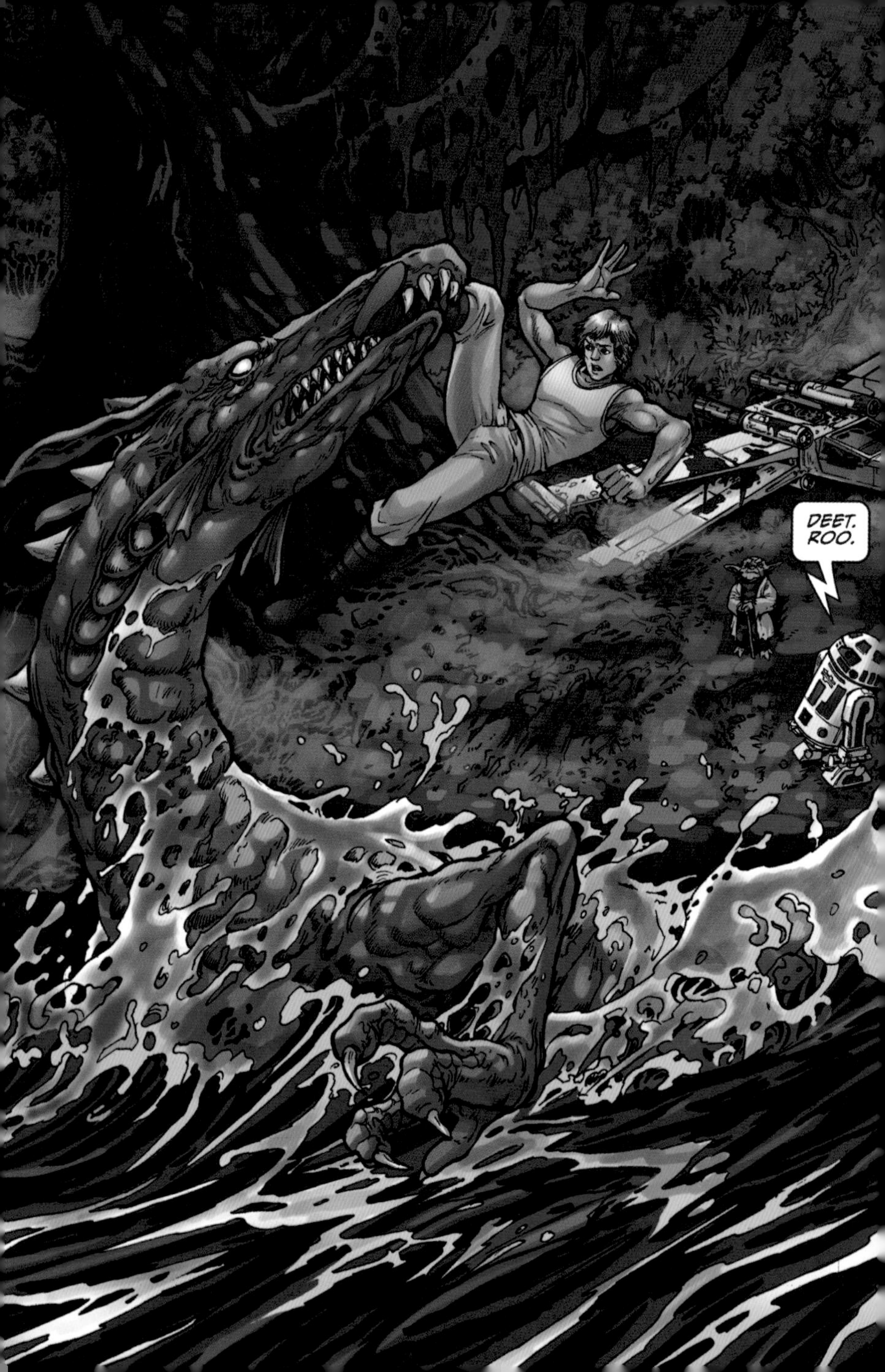
DEET. ROO.

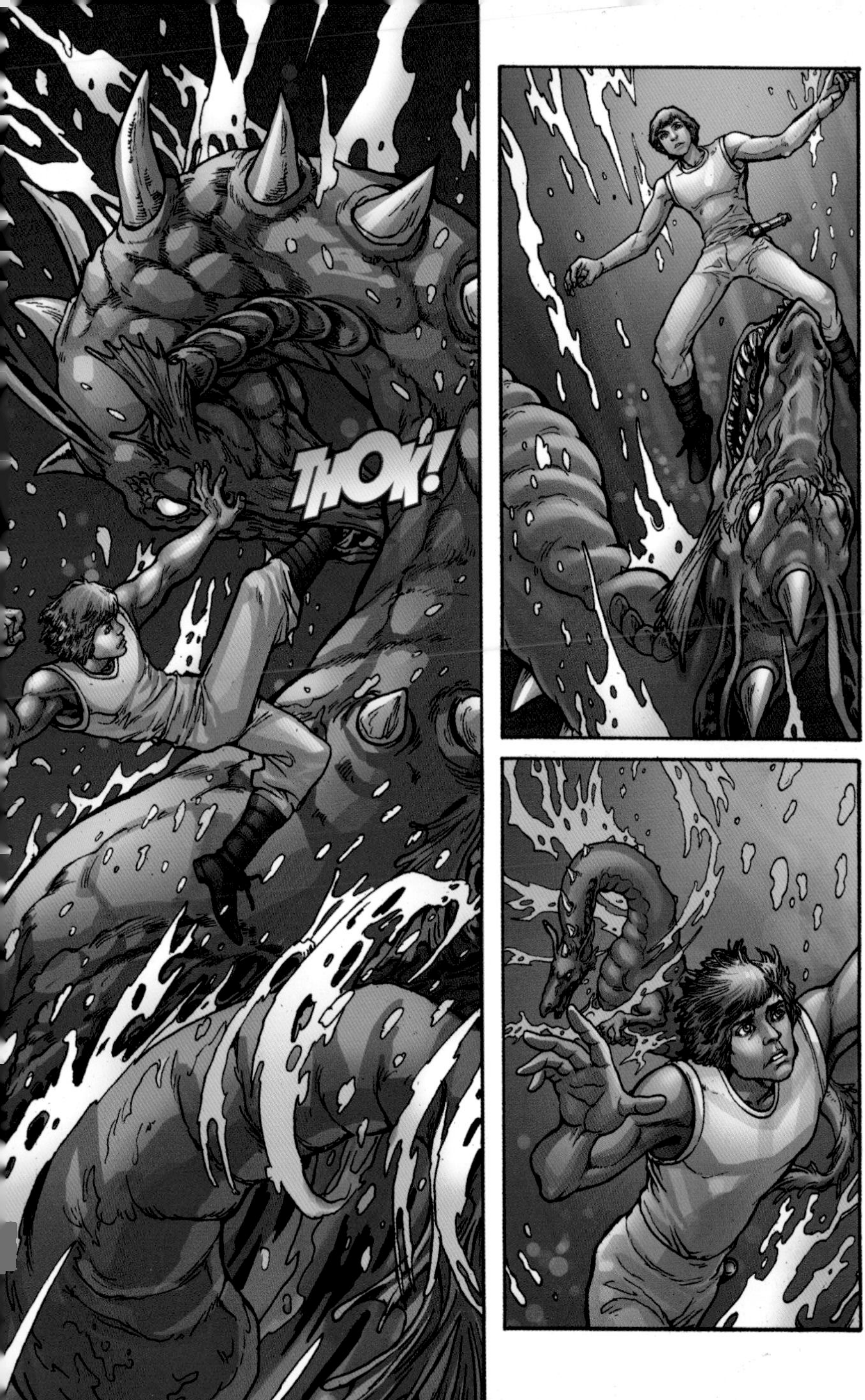
THOK!

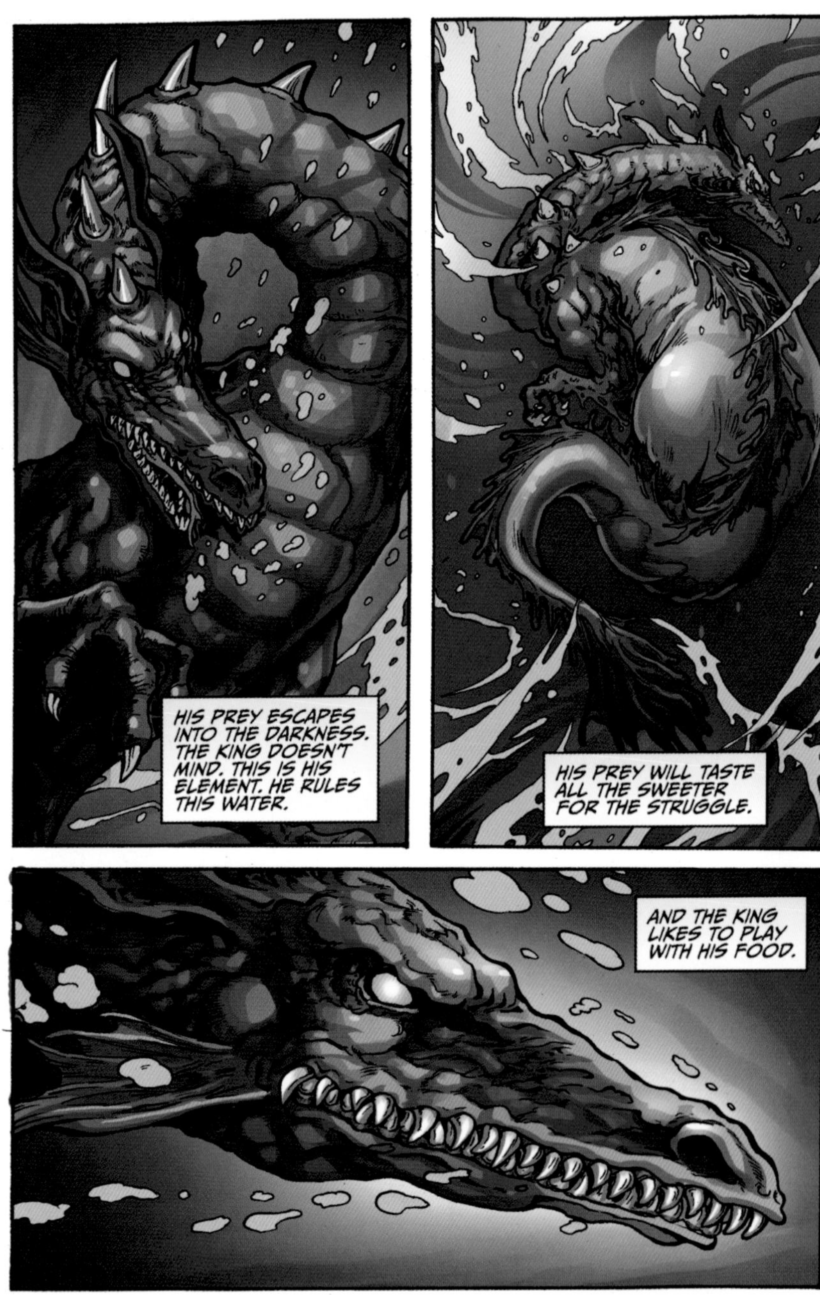
HIS PREY ESCAPES INTO THE DARKNESS. THE KING DOESN'T MIND. THIS IS HIS ELEMENT. HE RULES THIS WATER.
HIS PREY WILL TASTE ALL THE SWEETER FOR THE STRUGGLE.
AND THE KING LIKES TO PLAY WITH HIS FOOD.

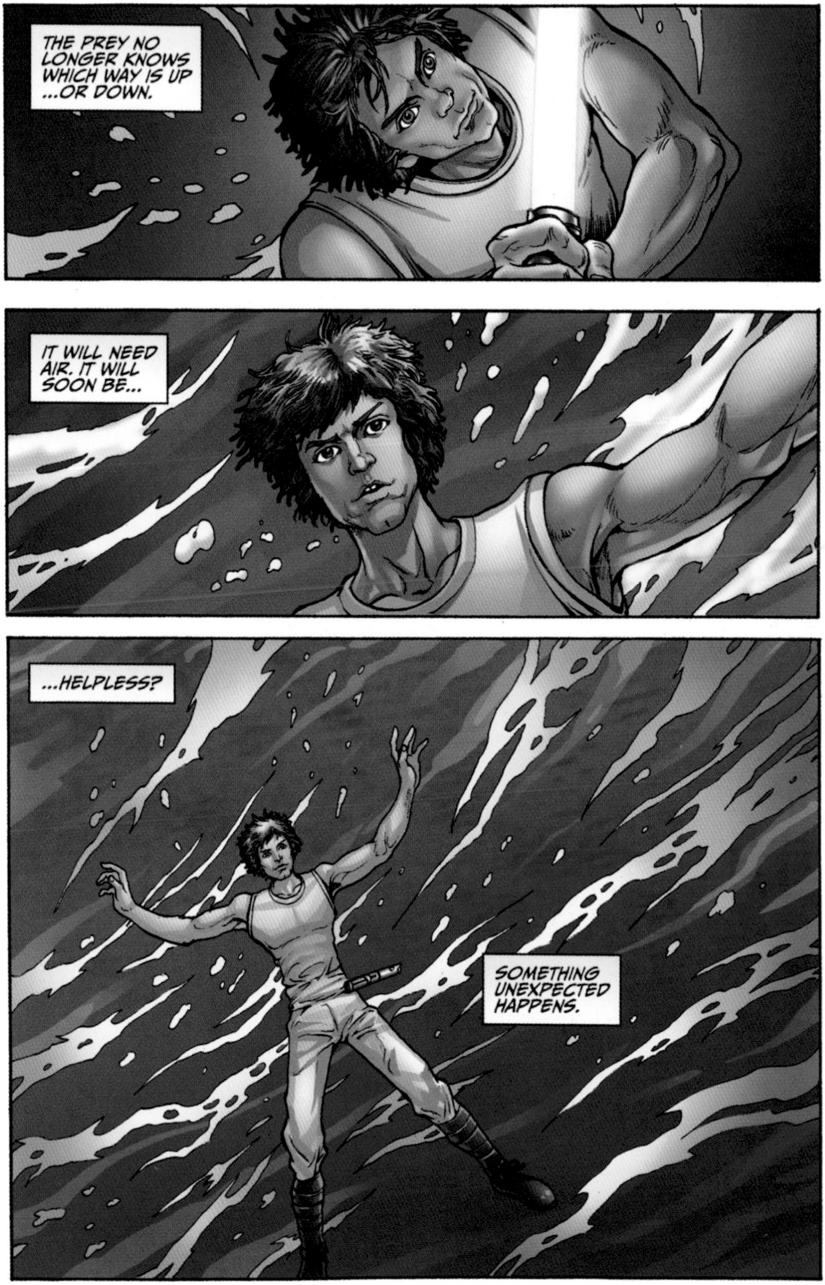
THE PREY NO LONGER KNOWS WHICH WAY IS UP ...OR DOWN.
IT WILL NEED AIR. IT WILL SOON BE...
...HELPLESS?
SOMETHING UNEXPECTED HAPPENS.

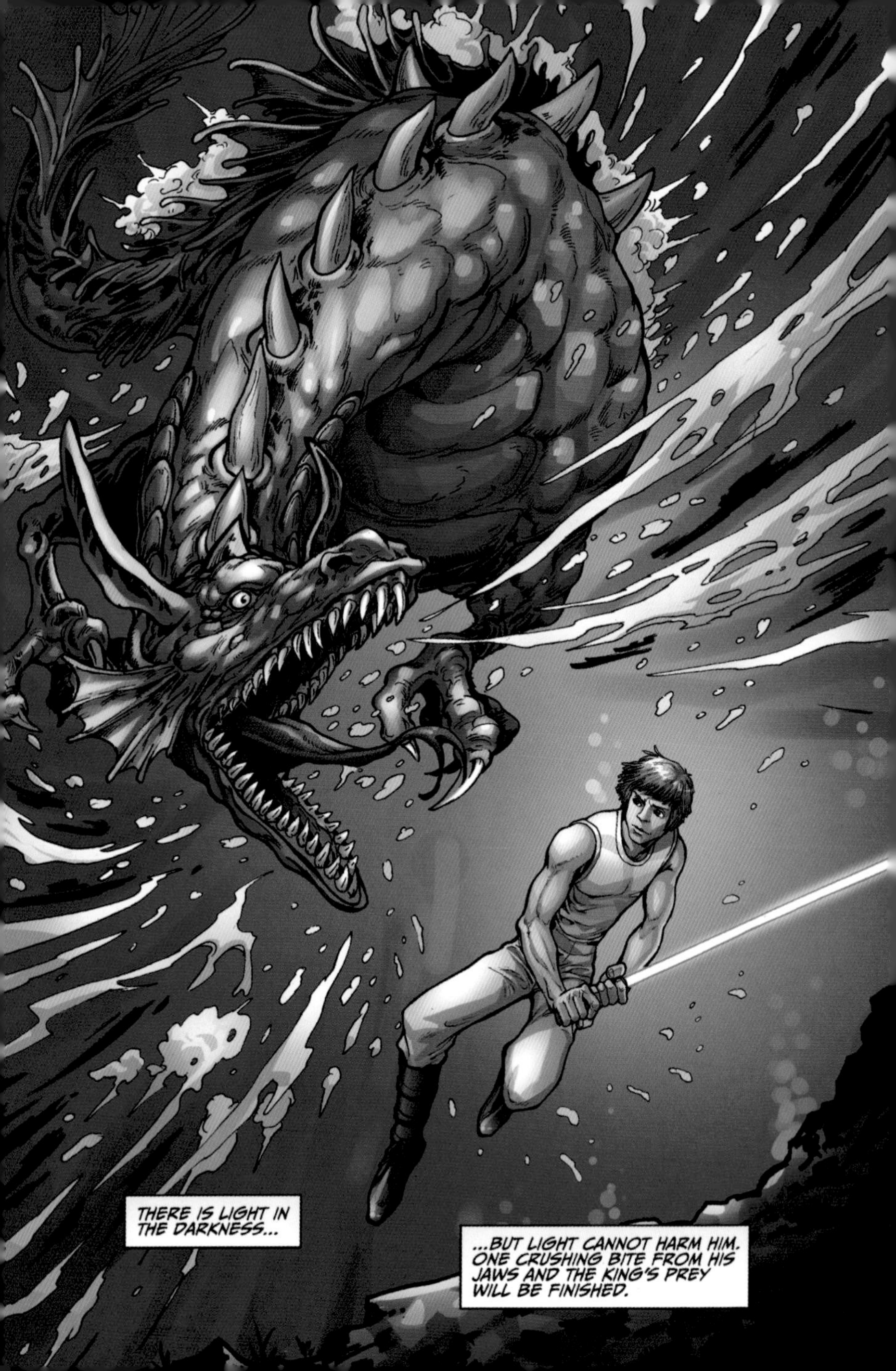
THERE IS LIGHT IN THE DARKNESS...
...BUT LIGHT CANNOT HARM HIM. ONE CRUSHING BITE FROM HIS JAWS AND THE KING'S PREY WILL BE FINISHED.

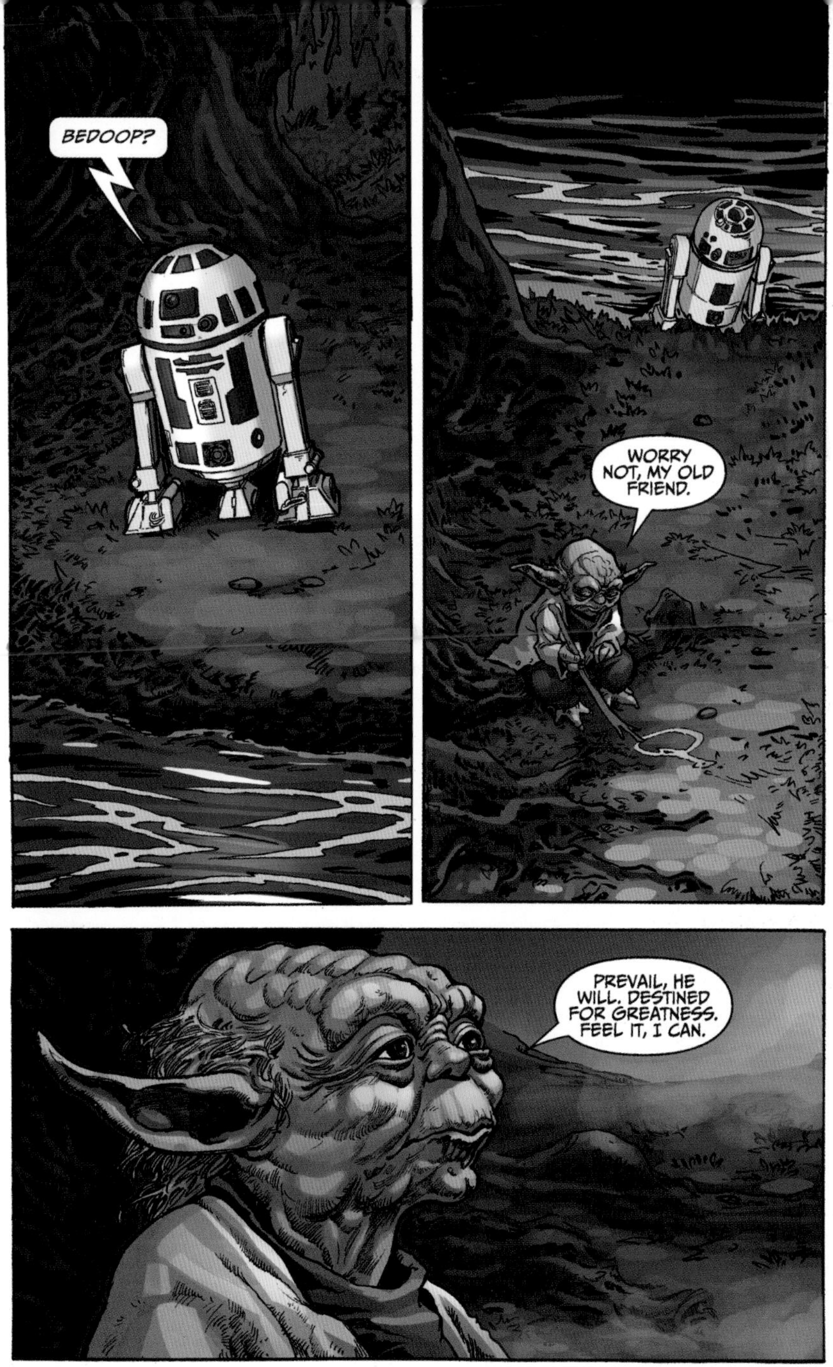
BEDOOP?
WORRY NOT, MY OLD FRIEND.
PREVAIL, HE WILL. DESTINED FOR GREATNESS. FEEL IT, I CAN.

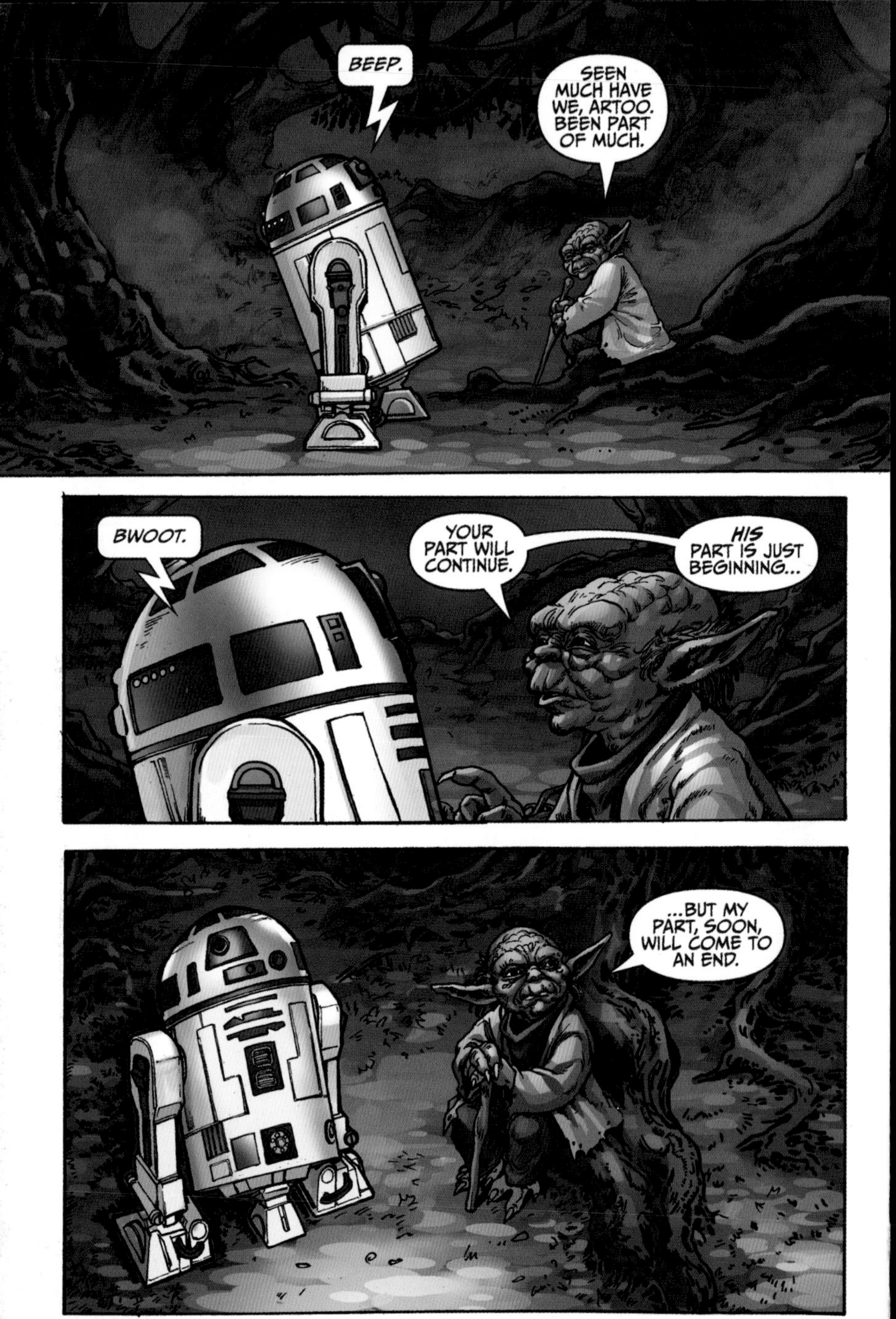
BEEP.
SEEN MUCH HAVE WE, ARTOO. BEEN PART OF MUCH.
BWOOT.
YOUR PART WILL CONTINUE.
HIS PART IS JUST BEGINNING...
...BUT MY PART, SOON, WILL COME TO AN END.

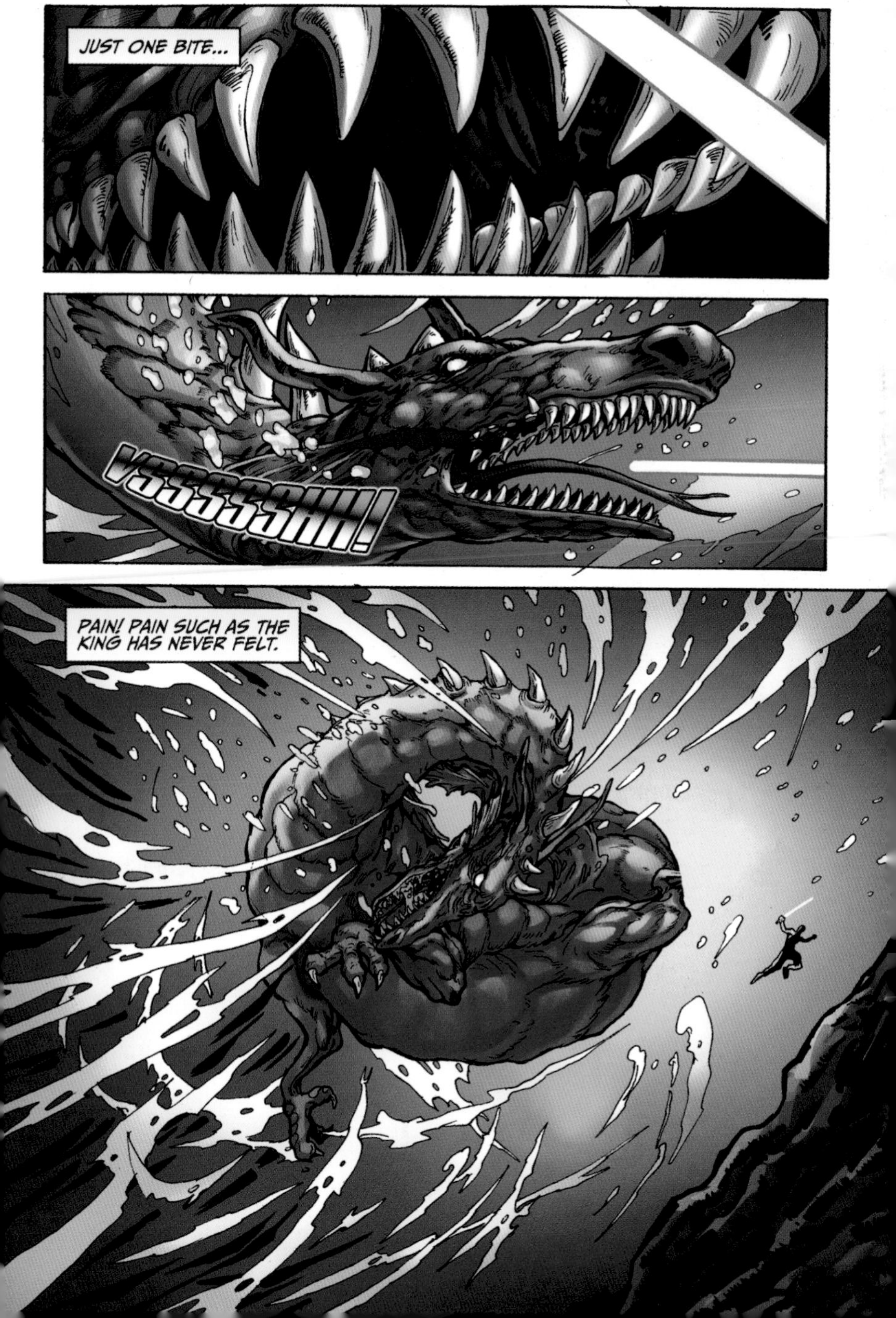
JUST ONE BITE...
VSSSSSSHH!
PAIN! PAIN SUCH AS THE KING HAS NEVER FELT.

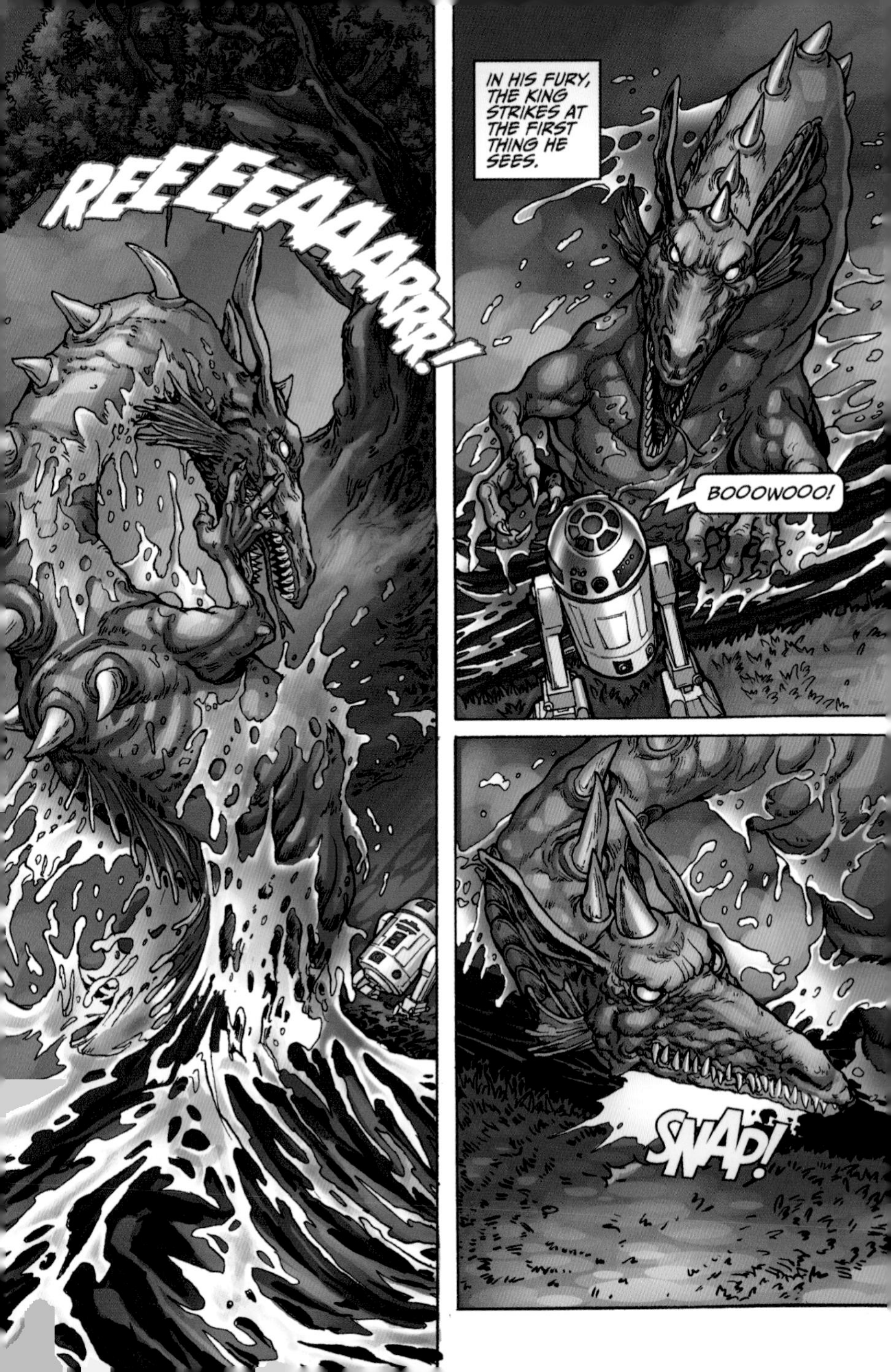
REEEEAAARRR!
IN HIS FURY, THE KING STRIKES AT THE FIRST THING HE SEES.
BOOOWOOO!
SNAP!

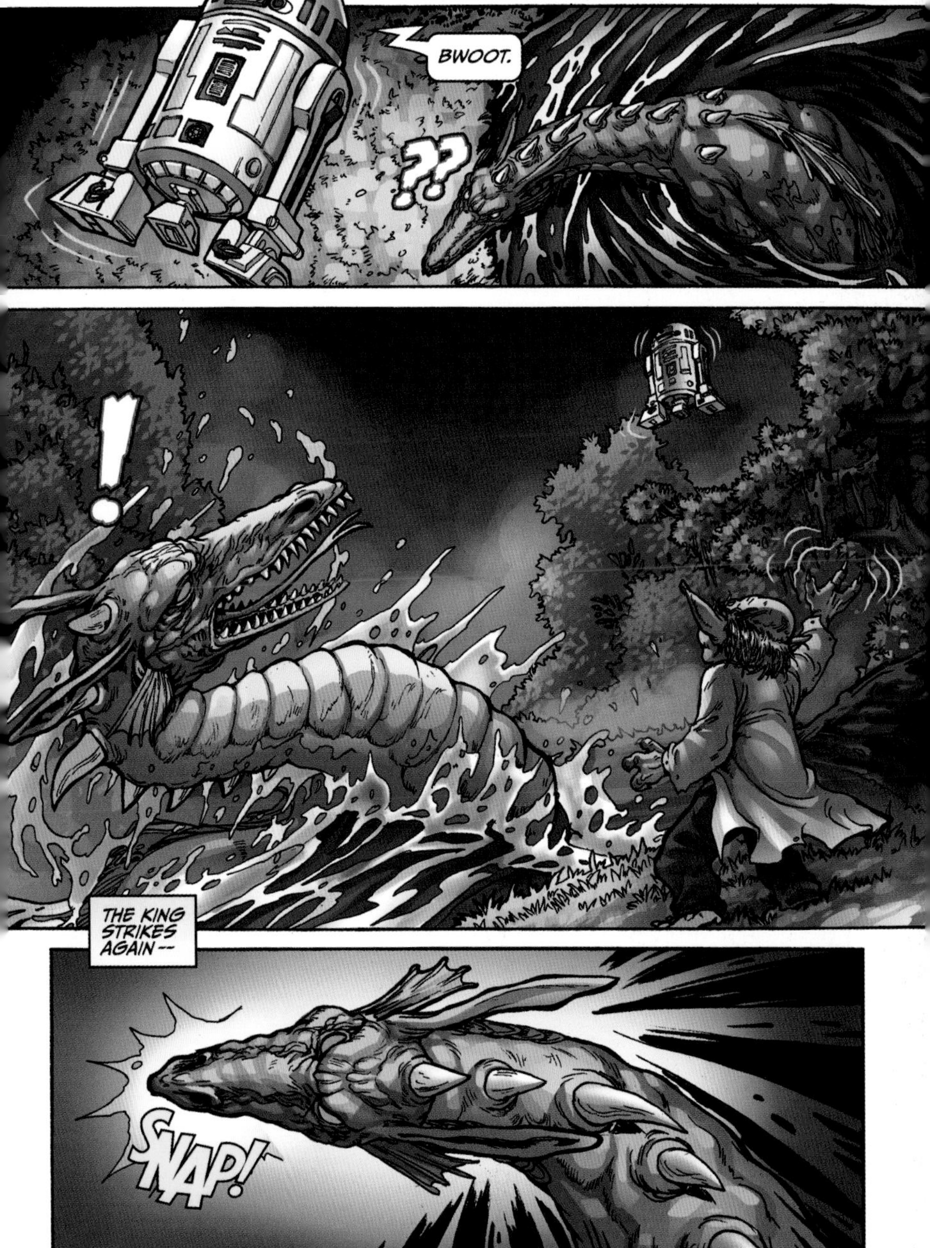
BWOOT.
??
!
THE KING STRIKES AGAIN--
SNAP!

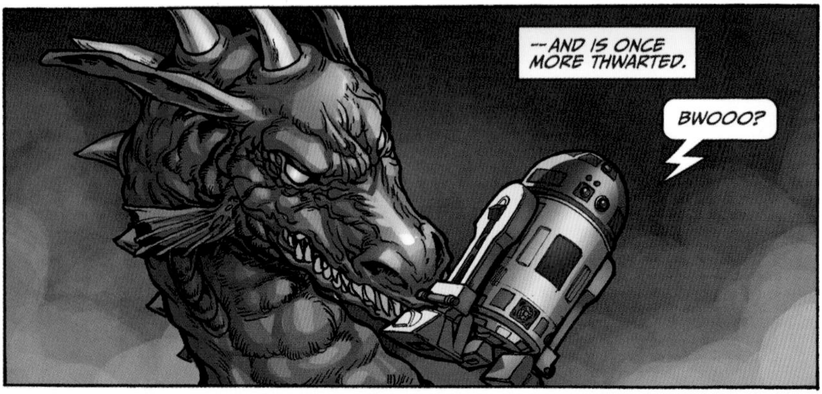
--AND IS ONCE MORE THWARTED.
BWOOO?

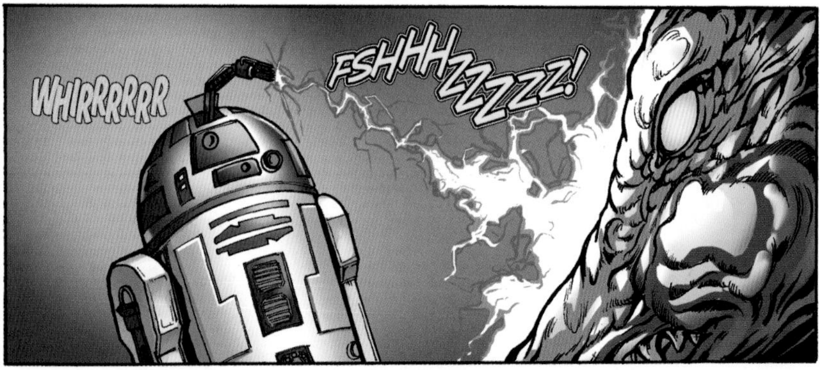
WHIRRRRRR
FSHHHZZZZZZ!

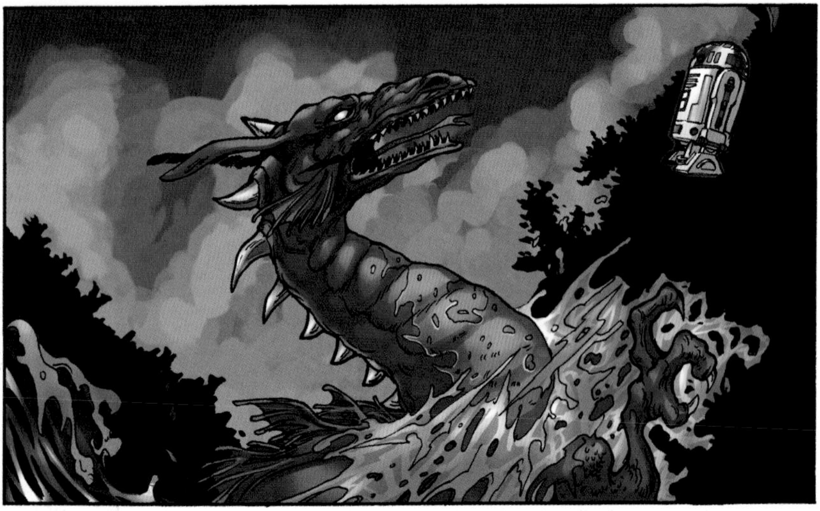

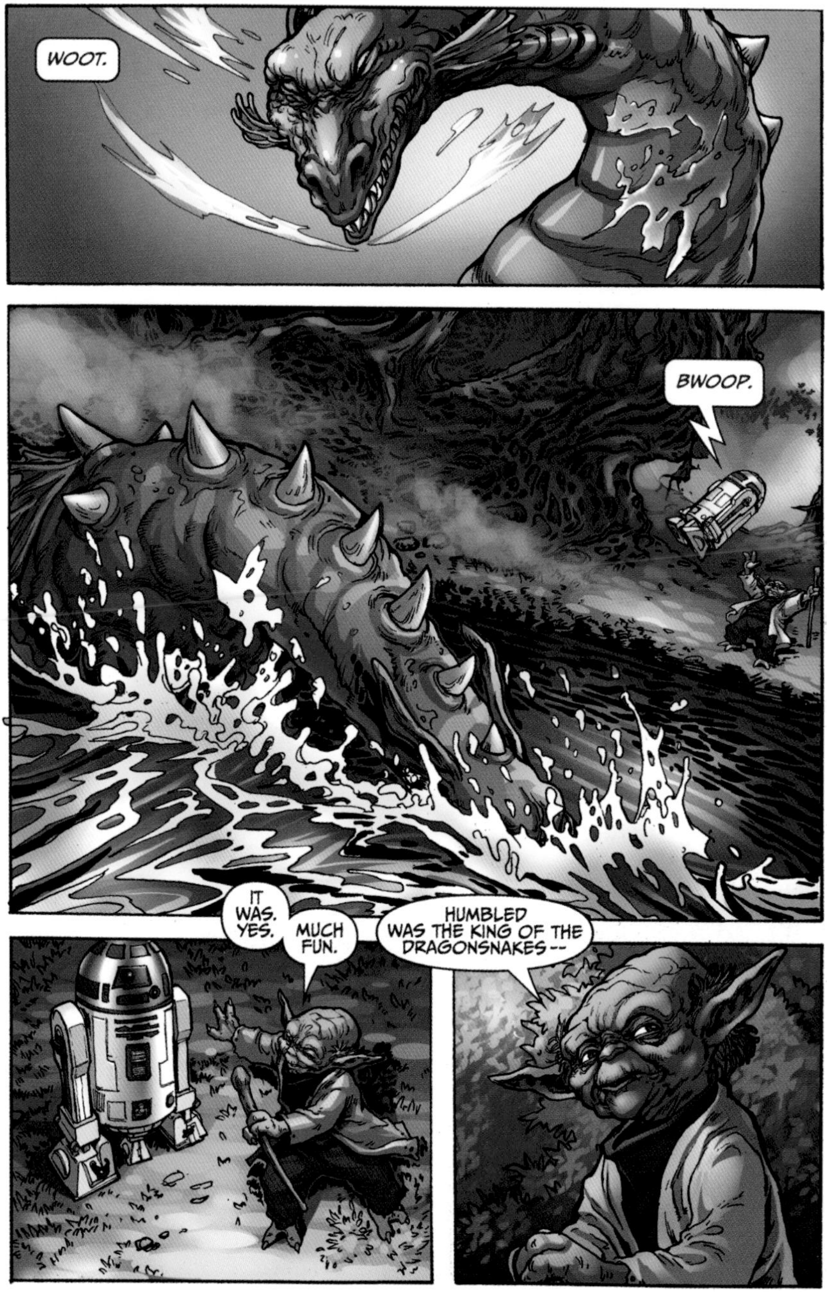
WOOT.
BWOOP.
IT WAS. YES.
MUCH FUN.
HUMBLED WAS THE KING OF THE DRAGONSNAKES --

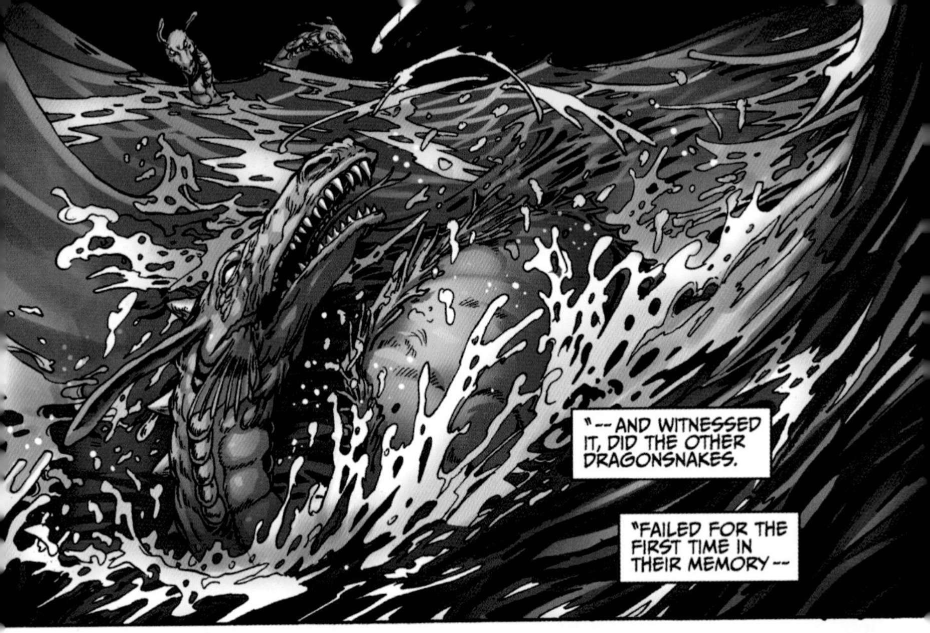
"--AND WITNESSED IT, DID THE OTHER DRAGONSNAKES.
"FAILED FOR THE FIRST TIME IN THEIR MEMORY--

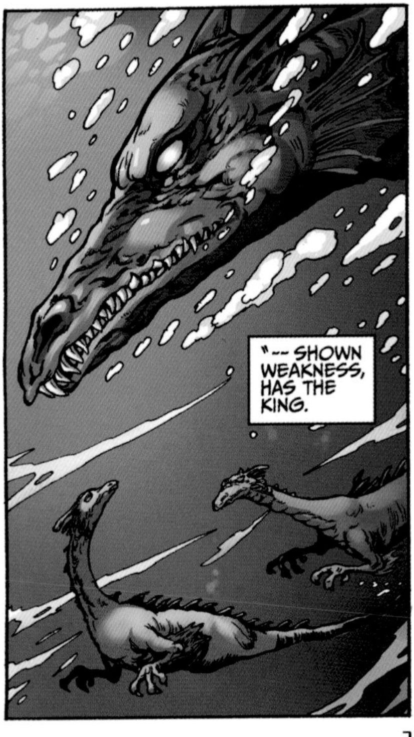
"--SHOWN WEAKNESS, HAS THE KING.

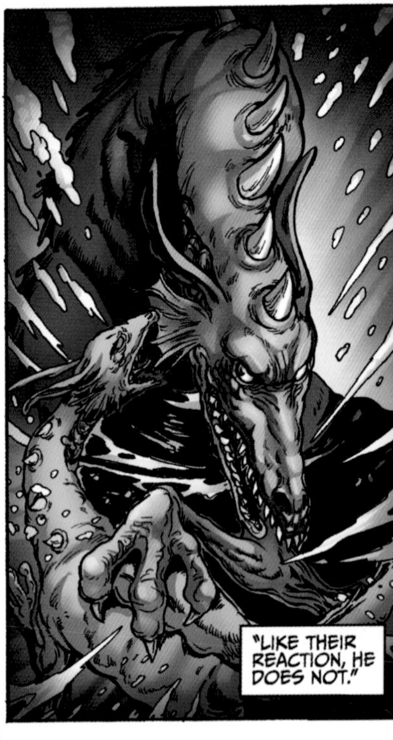
"LIKE THEIR REACTION, HE DOES NOT."

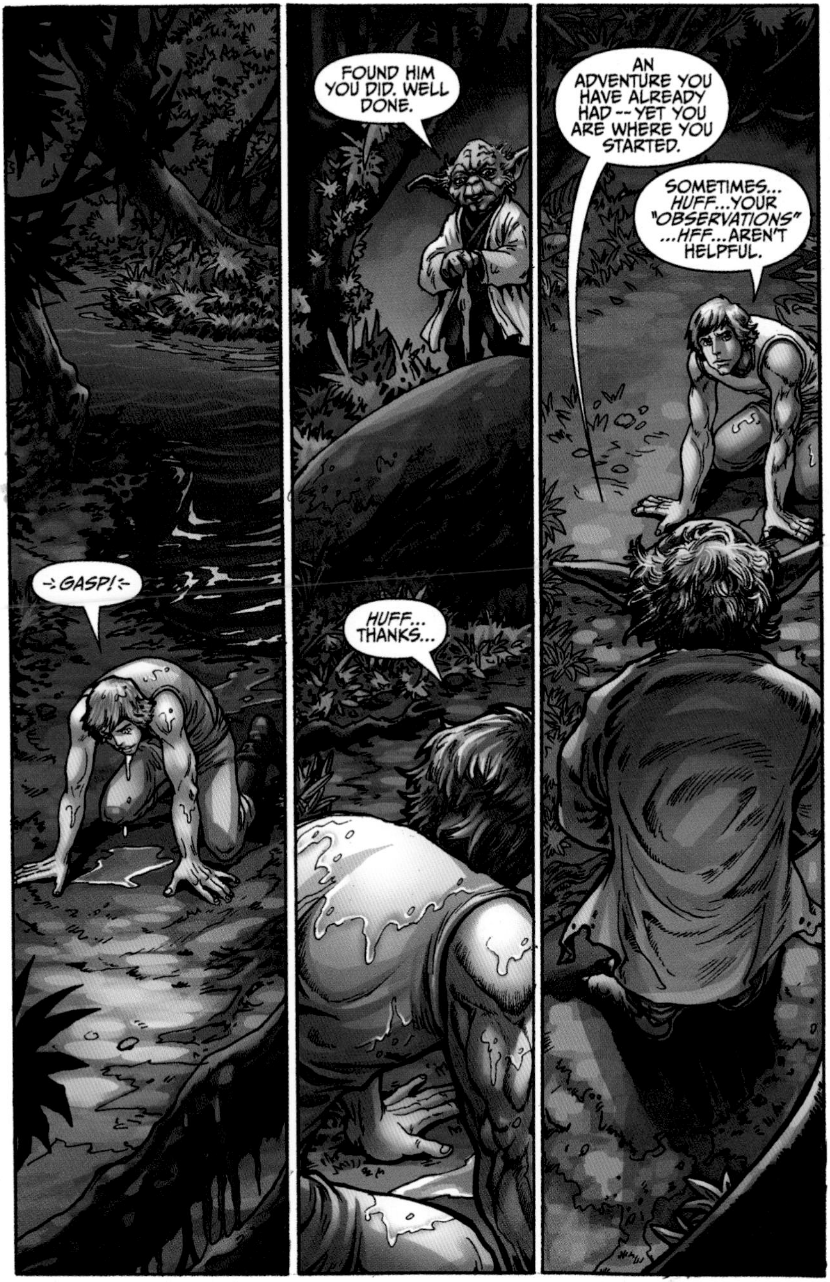
-GASP!-
FOUND HIM YOU DID. WELL DONE.
HUFF... THANKS...
AN ADVENTURE YOU HAVE ALREADY HAD -- YET YOU ARE WHERE YOU STARTED.
SOMETIMES... HUFF...YOUR "OBSERVATIONS" ...HFF...AREN'T HELPFUL.

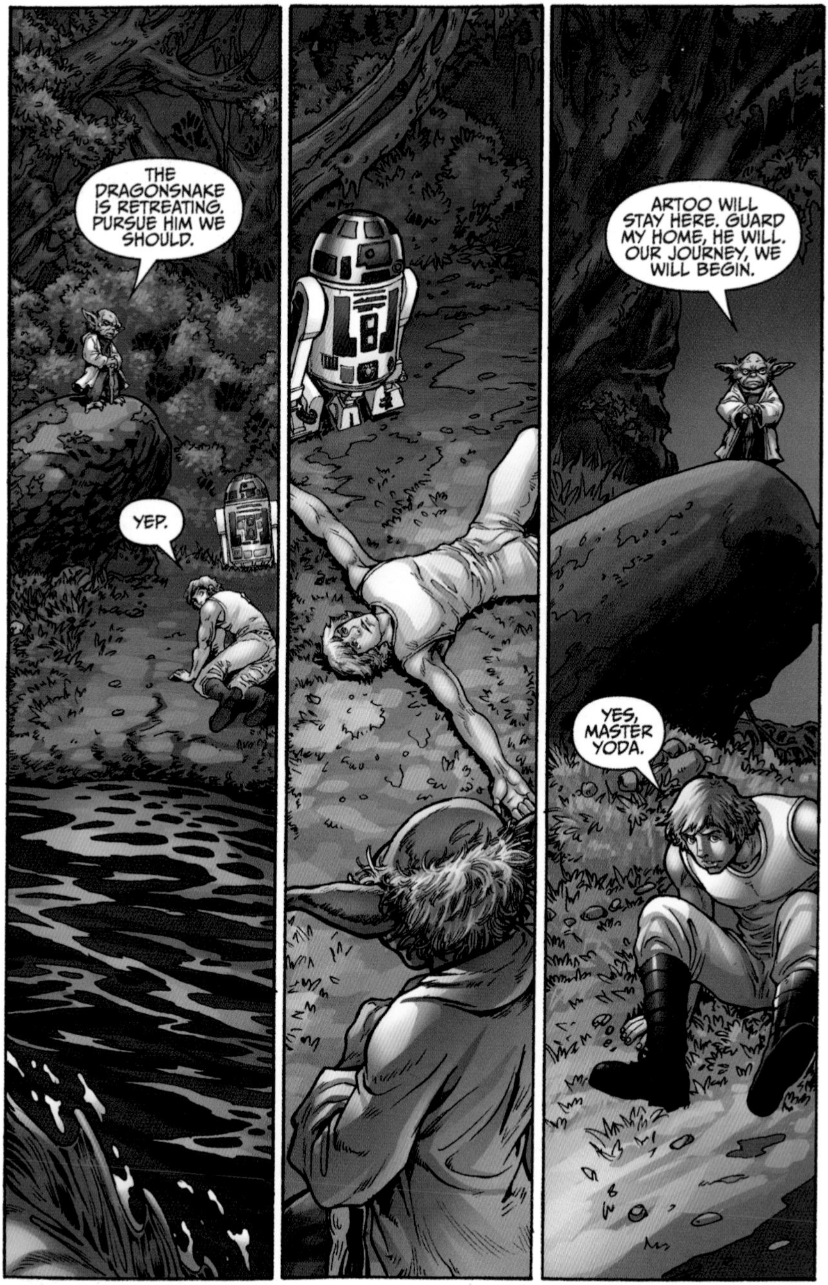
THE DRAGONSNAKE IS RETREATING. PURSUE HIM WE SHOULD.
YEP.
ARTOO WILL STAY HERE. GUARD MY HOME, HE WILL. OUR JOURNEY, WE WILL BEGIN.
YES, MASTER YODA.

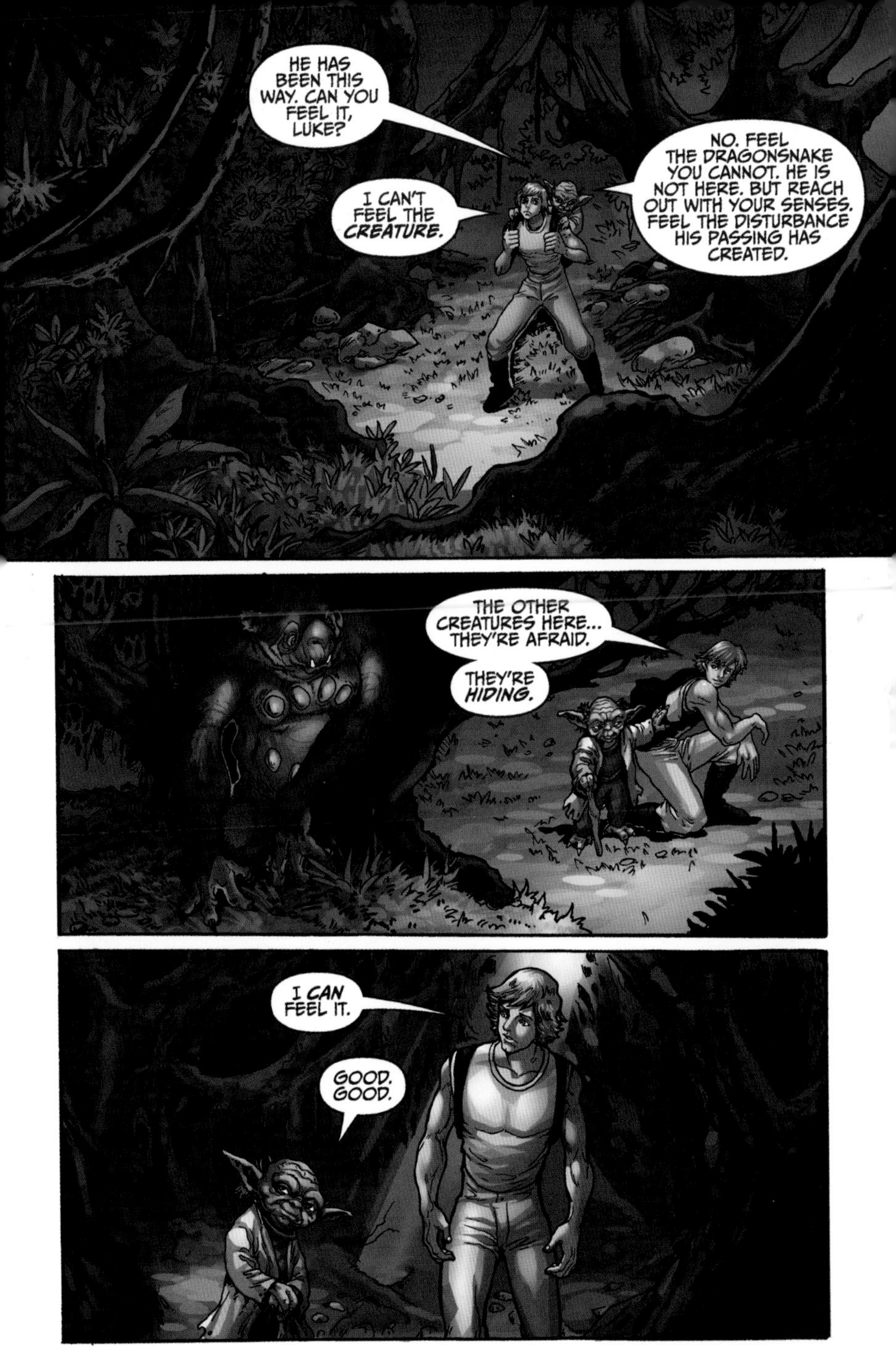
HE HAS BEEN THIS WAY. CAN YOU FEEL IT, LUKE?
I CAN'T FEEL THE CREATURE.
NO. FEEL THE DRAGONSNAKE YOU CANNOT. HE IS NOT HERE. BUT REACH OUT WITH YOUR SENSES. FEEL THE DISTURBANCE HIS PASSING HAS CREATED.
THE OTHER CREATURES HERE... THEY'RE AFRAID.
THEY'RE HIDING.
I CAN FEEL IT.
GOOD. GOOD.

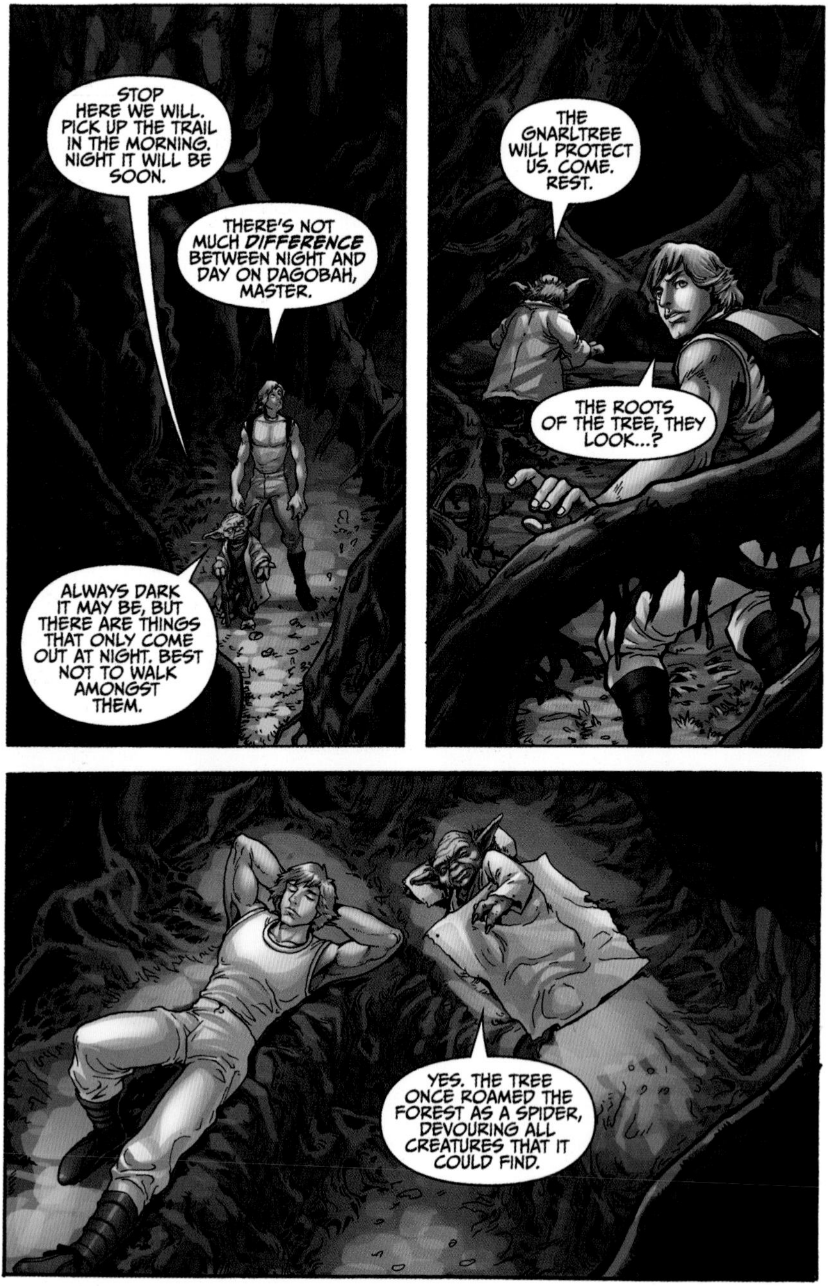
STOP HERE WE WILL. PICK UP THE TRAIL IN THE MORNING. NIGHT IT WILL BE SOON.
THERE'S NOT MUCH *DIFFERENCE* BETWEEN NIGHT AND DAY ON DAGOBAH, MASTER.
ALWAYS DARK IT MAY BE, BUT THERE ARE THINGS THAT ONLY COME OUT AT NIGHT. BEST NOT TO WALK AMONGST THEM.
THE GNARLTREE WILL PROTECT US. COME. REST.
THE ROOTS OF THE TREE, THEY LOOK...?
YES. THE TREE ONCE ROAMED THE FOREST AS A SPIDER, DEVOURING ALL CREATURES THAT IT COULD FIND.

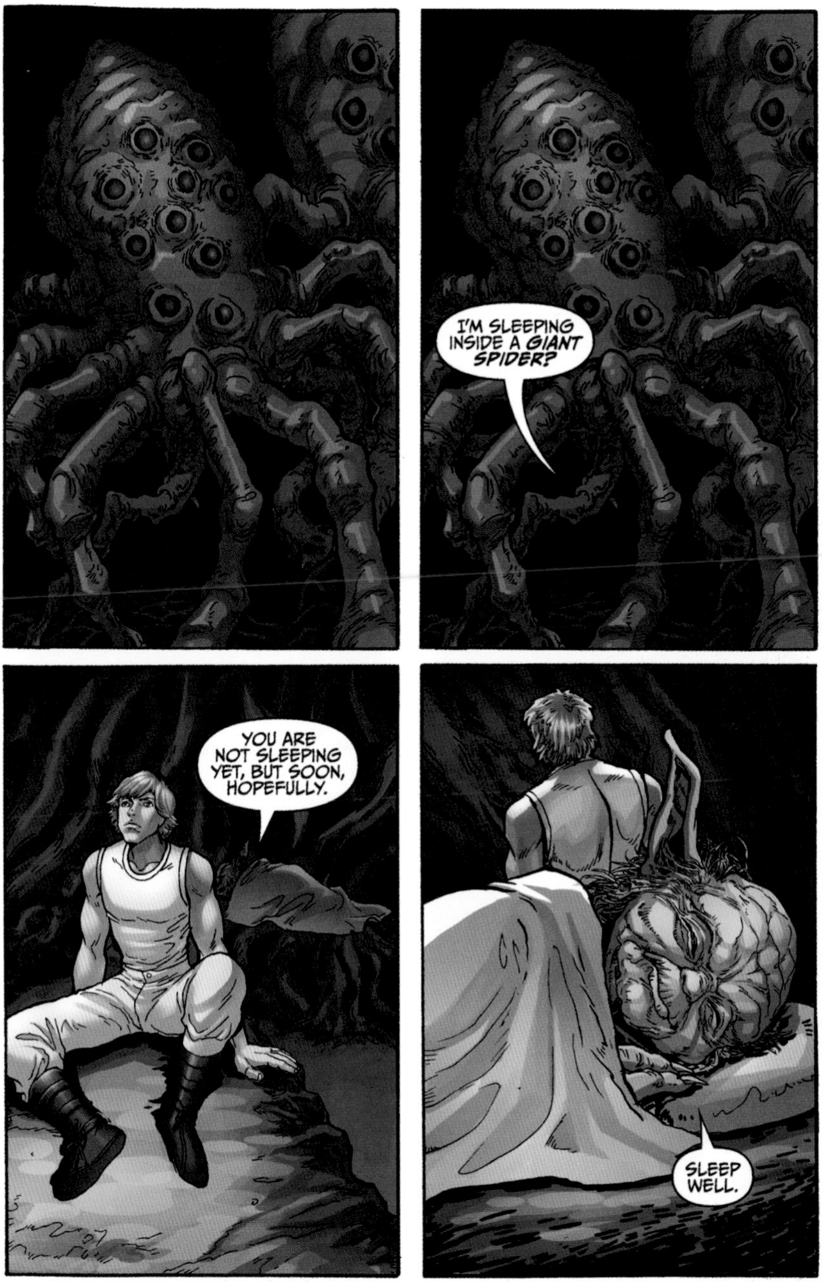
I'M SLEEPING INSIDE A *GIANT* SPIDER?
YOU ARE NOT SLEEPING YET, BUT SOON, HOPEFULLY.
SLEEP WELL.

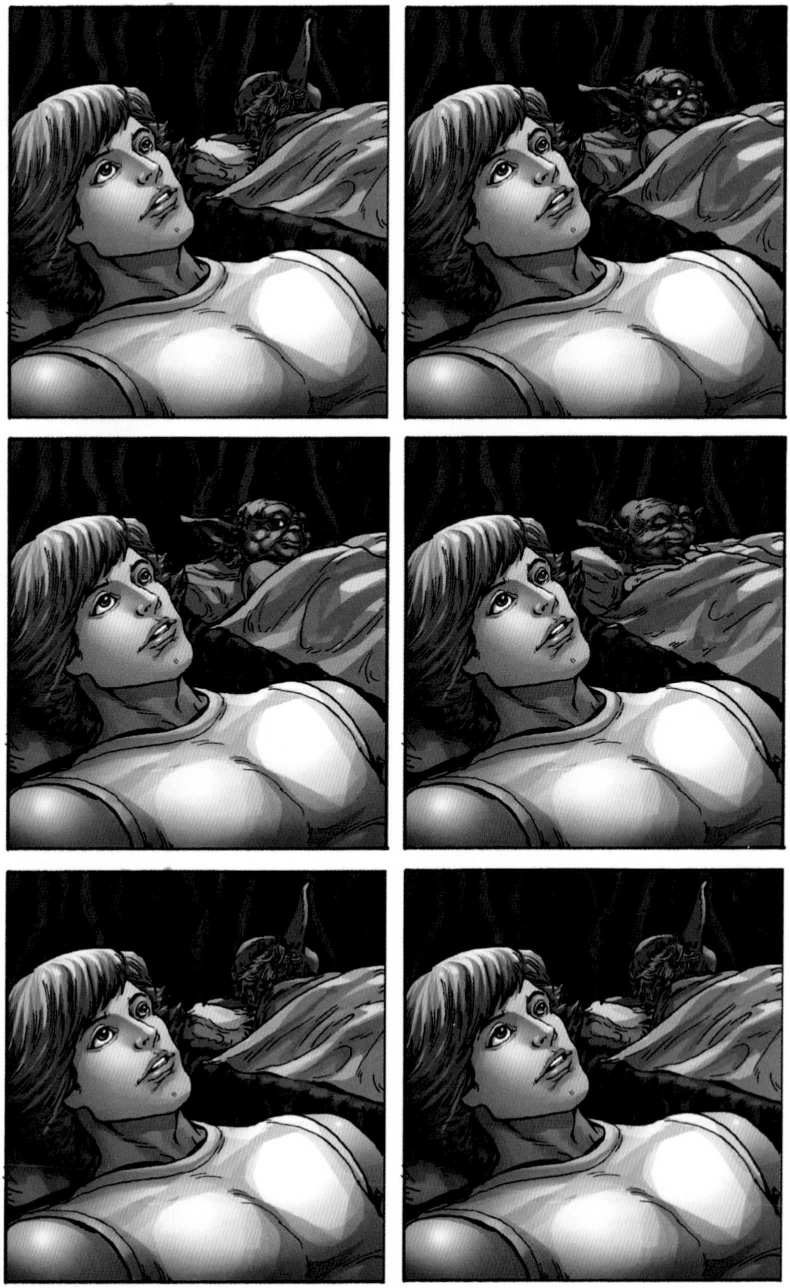

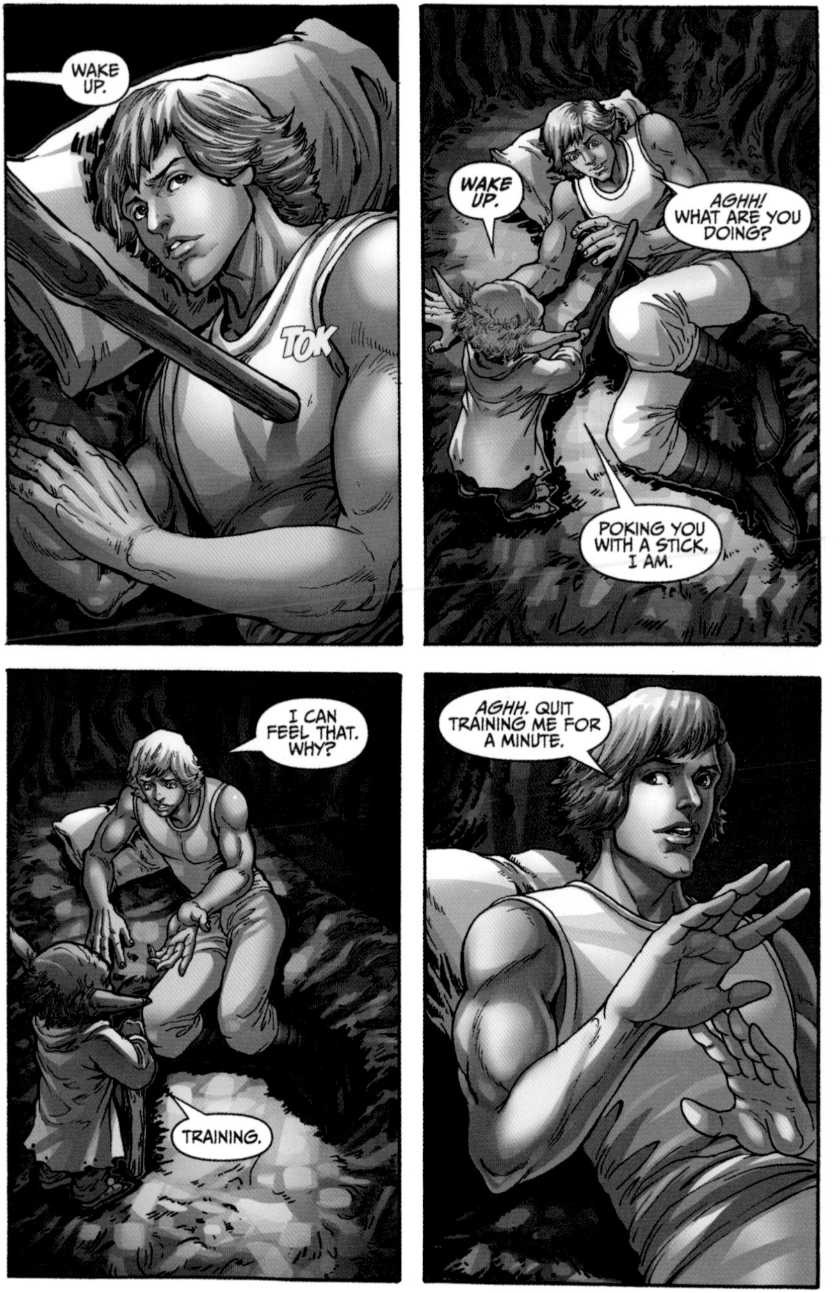
WAKE UP.
TOK
WAKE UP.
AGHH! WHAT ARE YOU DOING?
POKING YOU WITH A STICK, I AM.
I CAN FEEL THAT. WHY?
TRAINING.
AGHH. QUIT TRAINING ME FOR A MINUTE.

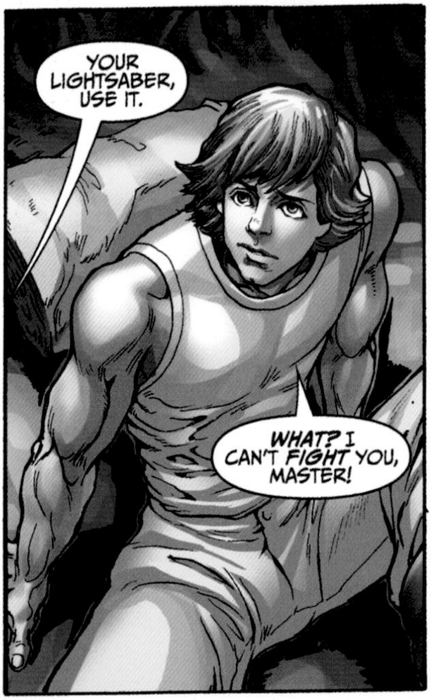
YOUR LIGHTSABER, USE IT.
WHAT? I CAN'T FIGHT YOU, MASTER!

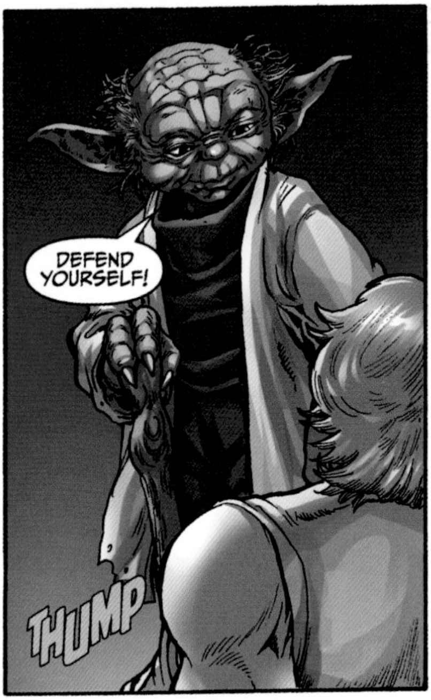
DEFEND YOURSELF!
THUMP

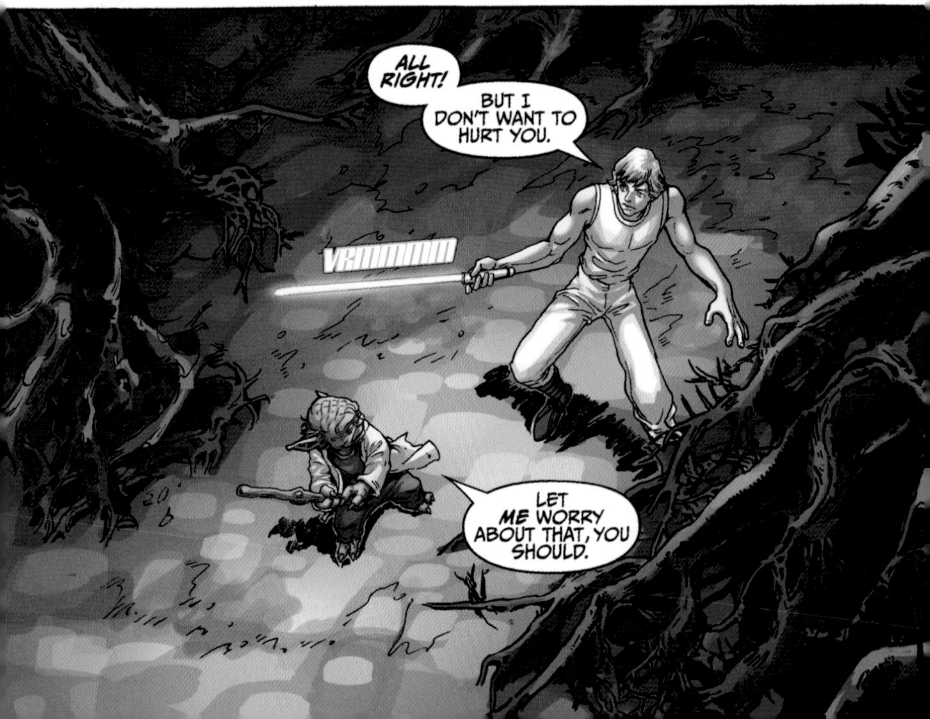
ALL RIGHT!
BUT I DON'T WANT TO HURT YOU.
VRMMMM
LET ME WORRY ABOUT THAT, YOU SHOULD.

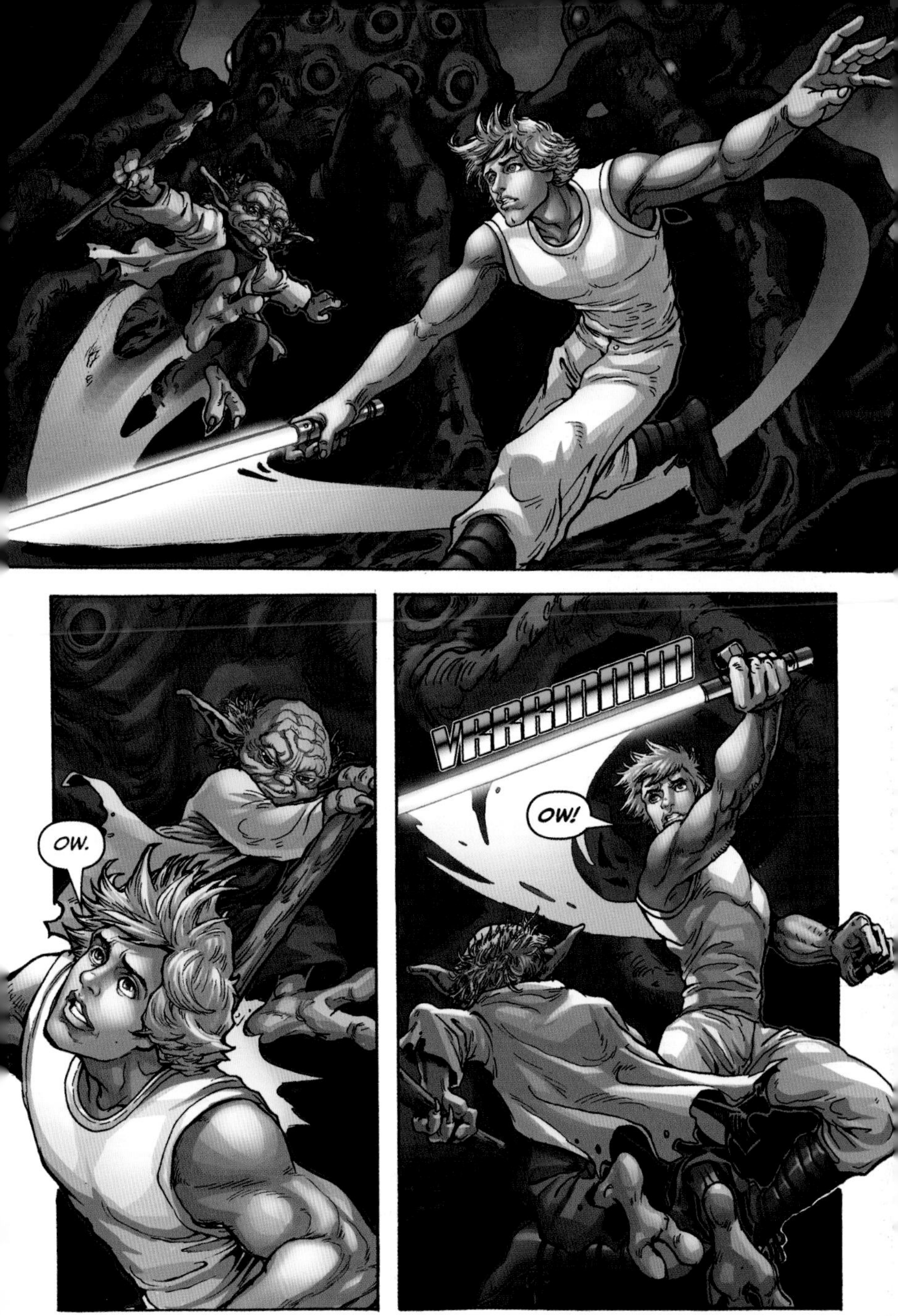
OW.
VRRMMMM
OW!

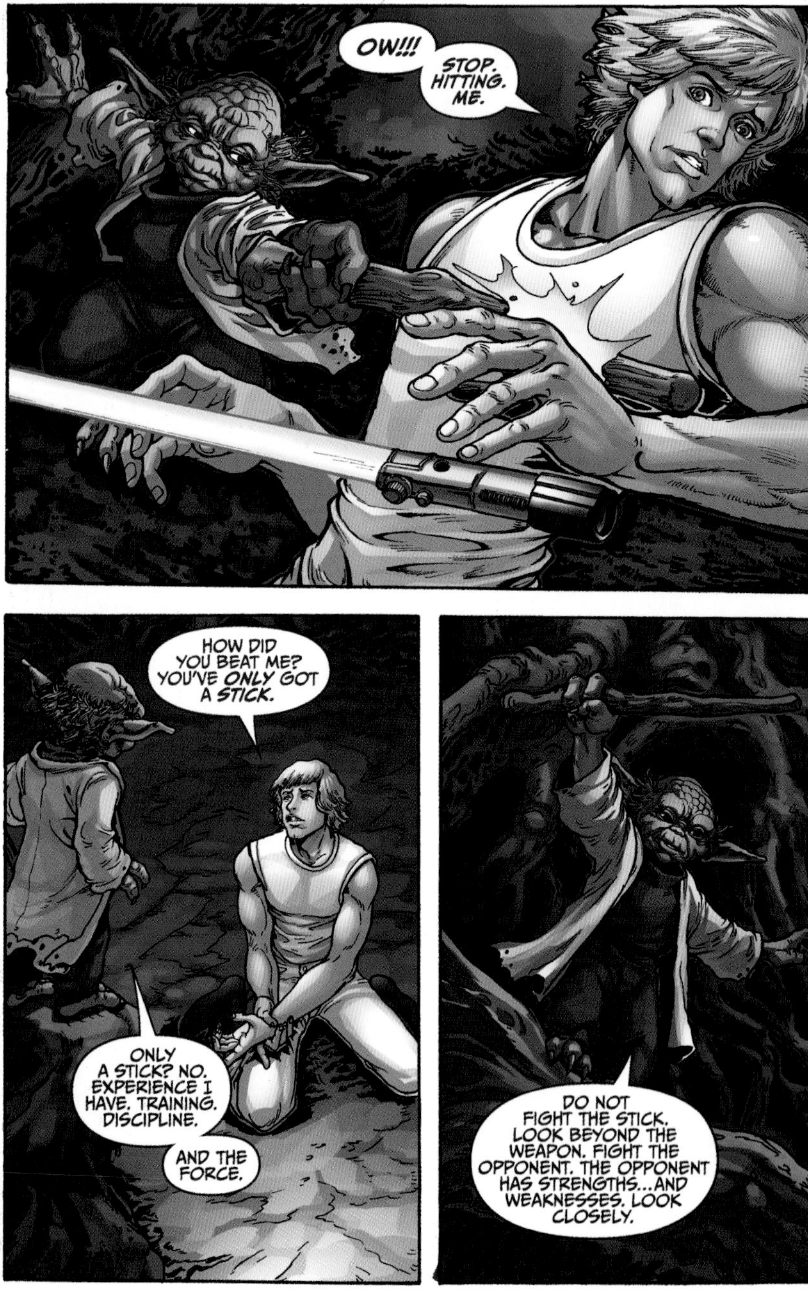
OW!!!
STOP. HITTING. ME.
HOW DID YOU BEAT ME? YOU'VE ONLY GOT A STICK.
ONLY A STICK? NO. EXPERIENCE I HAVE. TRAINING. DISCIPLINE.
AND THE FORCE.
DO NOT FIGHT THE STICK. LOOK BEYOND THE WEAPON. FIGHT THE OPPONENT. THE OPPONENT HAS STRENGTHS...AND WEAKNESSES. LOOK CLOSELY.

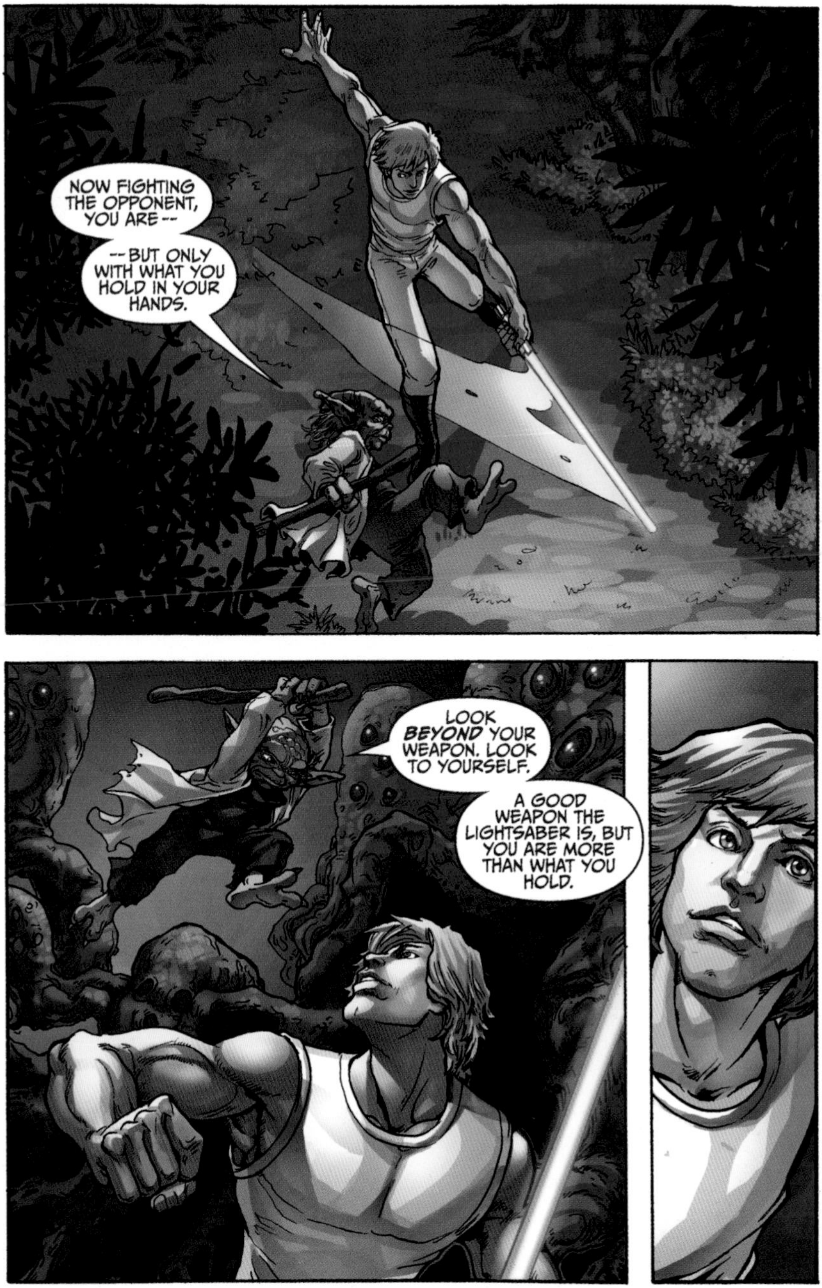
NOW FIGHTING THE OPPONENT, YOU ARE --
-- BUT ONLY WITH WHAT YOU HOLD IN YOUR HANDS.
LOOK *BEYOND* YOUR WEAPON. LOOK TO YOURSELF.
A GOOD WEAPON THE LIGHTSABER IS, BUT YOU ARE MORE THAN WHAT YOU HOLD.

HNGH.

VRRRRRRIIIIIIIRRRIIIII

HA!

I DID IT!

HMMPH... ONLY BEAT A STICK YOU DID.

COME--

48

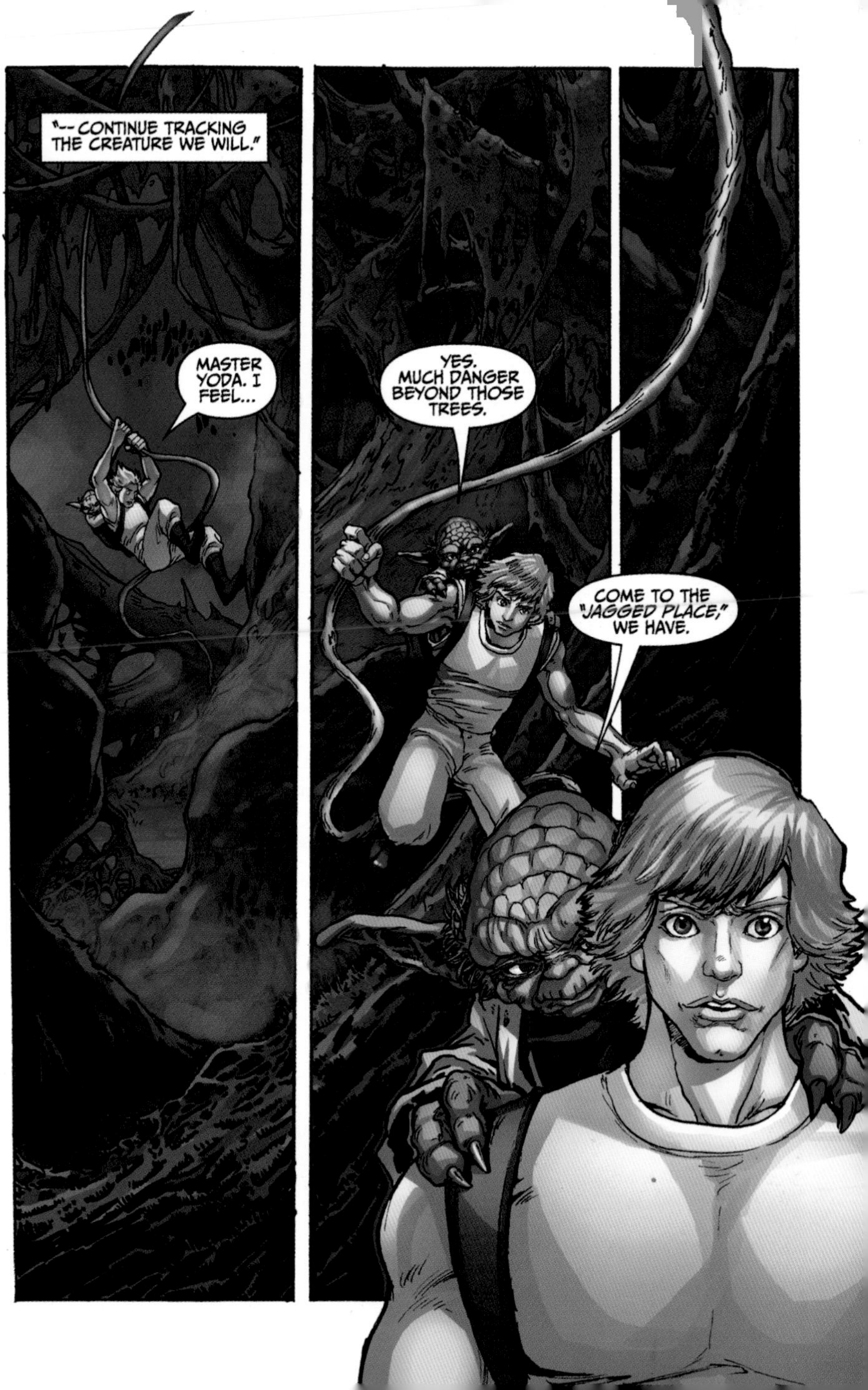
"-- CONTINUE TRACKING THE CREATURE WE WILL."
MASTER YODA. I FEEL...
YES. MUCH DANGER BEYOND THOSE TREES.
COME TO THE "JAGGED PLACE," WE HAVE.

THE DISTURBANCE LEFT BY THE DRAGON-SNAKE...

...I CAN'T *FEEL* IT ANYMORE.

NO.

ALL IS DISTURBED HERE.

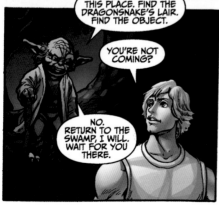

LINGER NOT IN THIS PLACE. FIND THE DRAGONSNAKE'S LAIR. FIND THE OBJECT.

YOU'RE NOT COMING?

NO. RETURN TO THE SWAMP, I WILL. WAIT FOR YOU THERE.

NO FURTHER WILL I GO.

THIS PART OF THE JOURNEY, LUKE, IS YOURS ALONE.

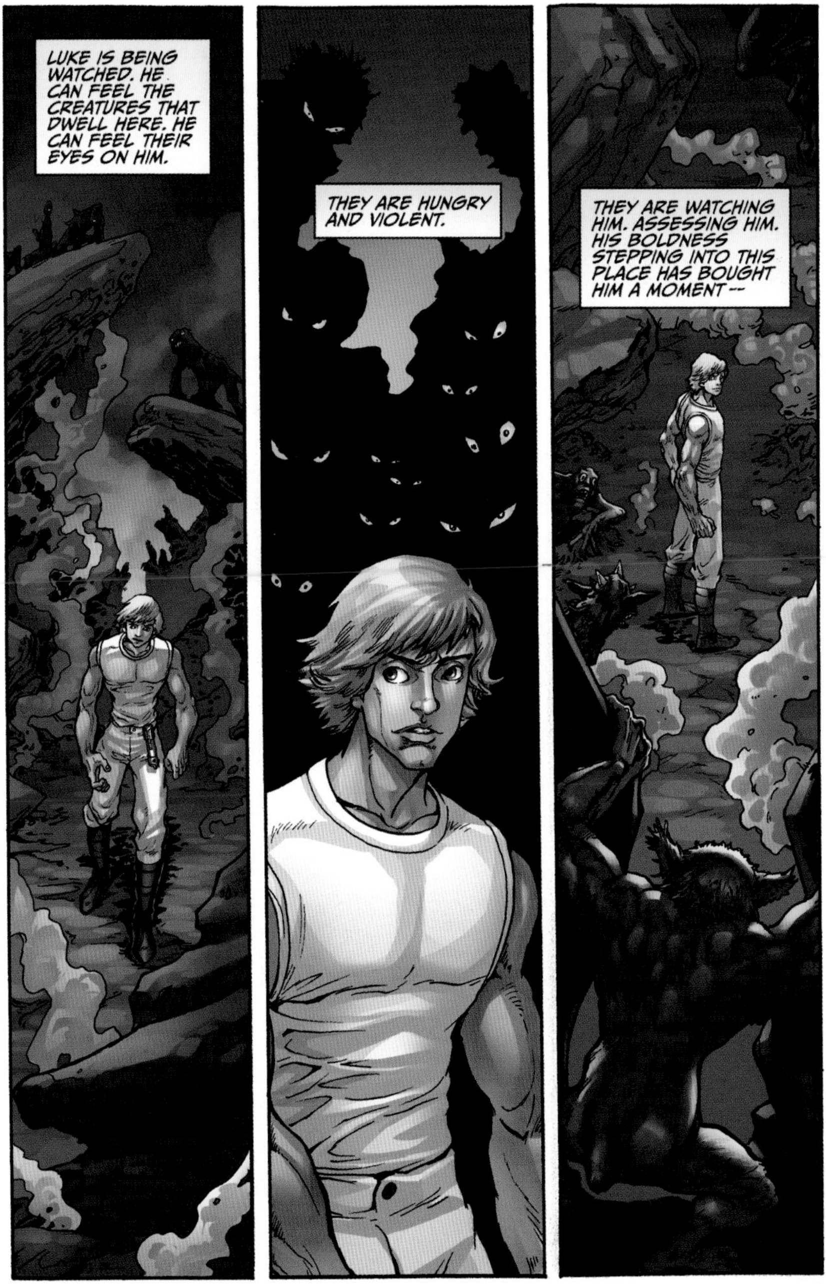
LUKE IS BEING WATCHED. HE CAN FEEL THE CREATURES THAT DWELL HERE. HE CAN FEEL THEIR EYES ON HIM.
THEY ARE HUNGRY AND VIOLENT.
THEY ARE WATCHING HIM. ASSESSING HIM. HIS BOLDNESS STEPPING INTO THIS PLACE HAS BOUGHT HIM A MOMENT--

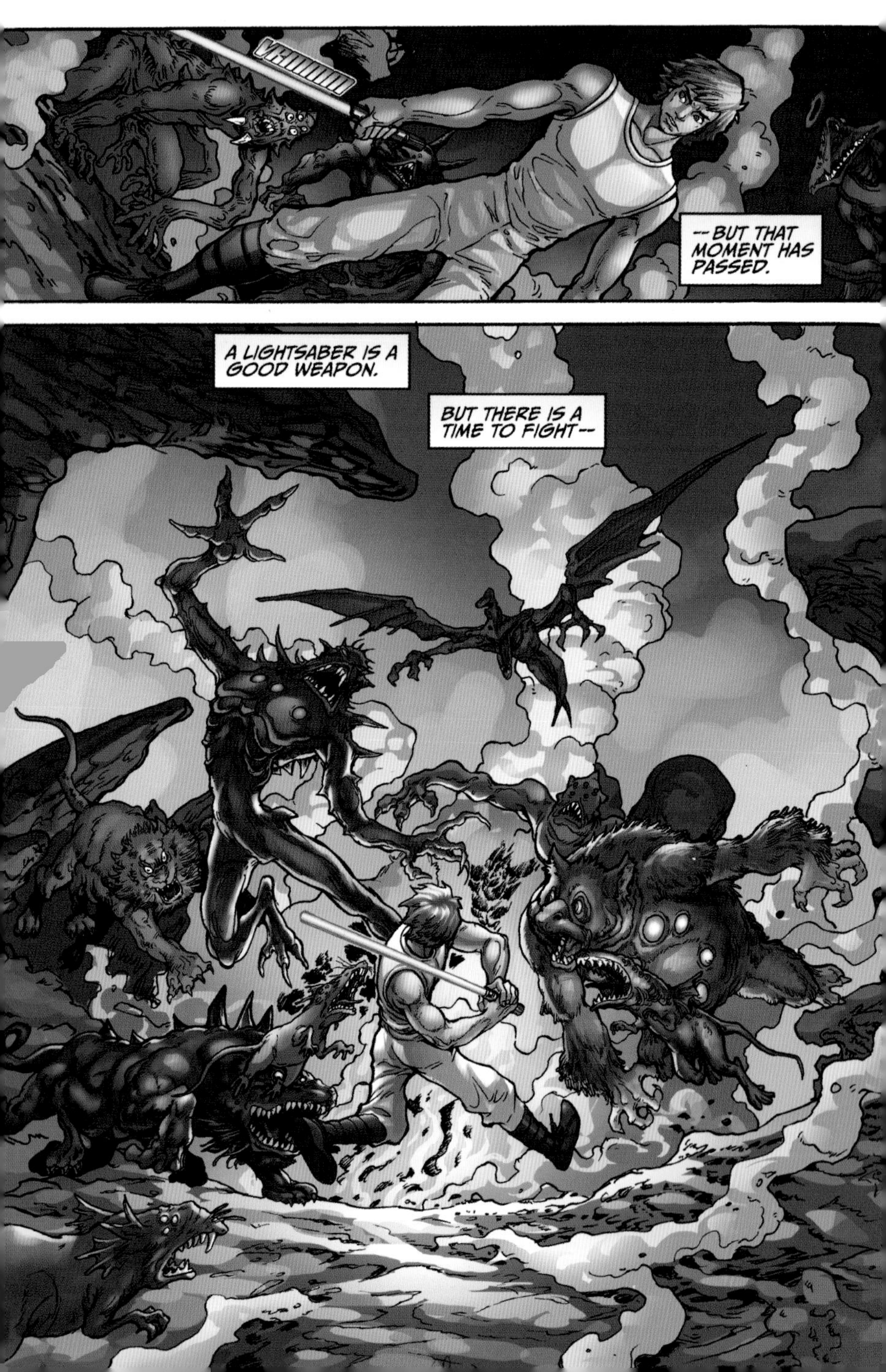
--BUT THAT MOMENT HAS PASSED.
A LIGHTSABER IS A GOOD WEAPON.
BUT THERE IS A TIME TO FIGHT--

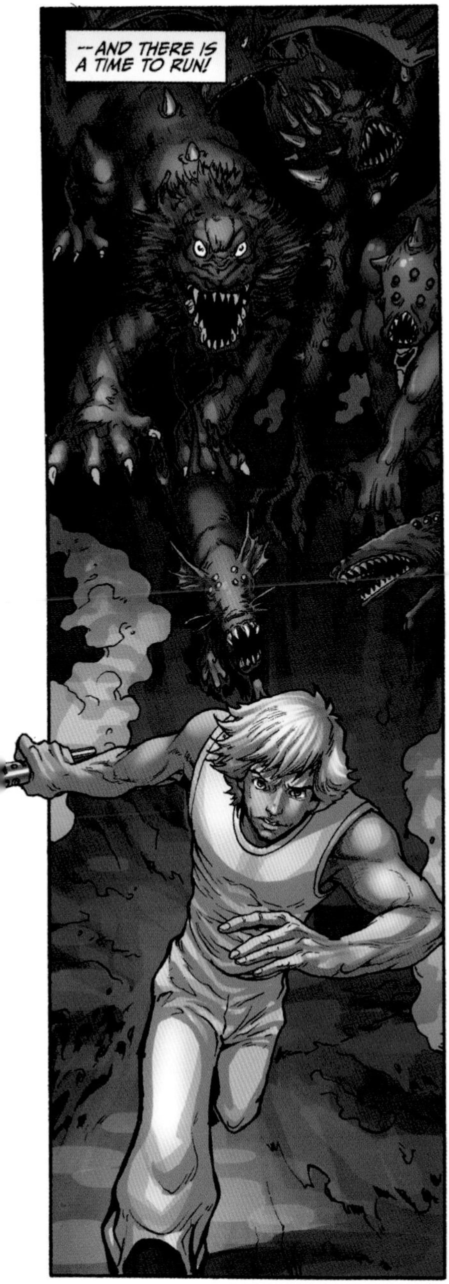
--AND THERE IS A TIME TO RUN!

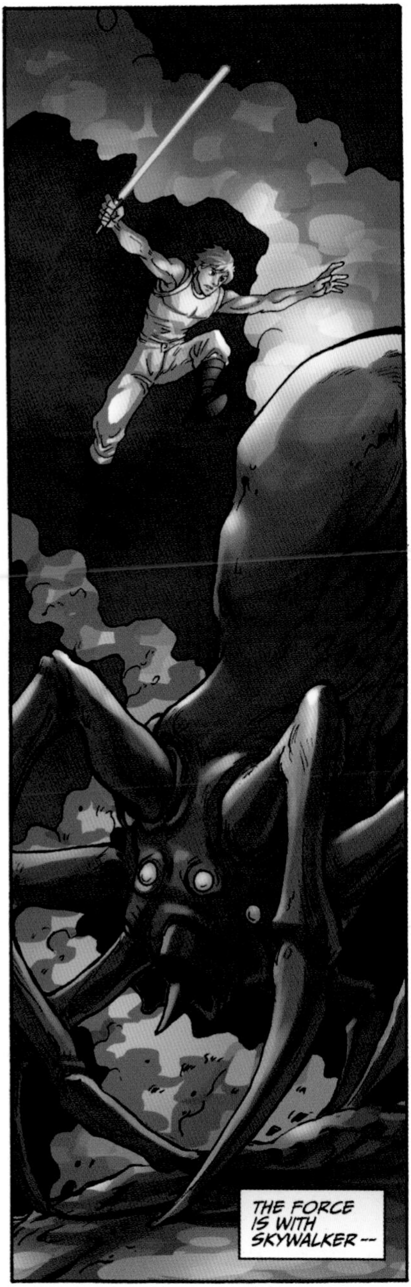
THE FORCE IS WITH SKYWALKER--

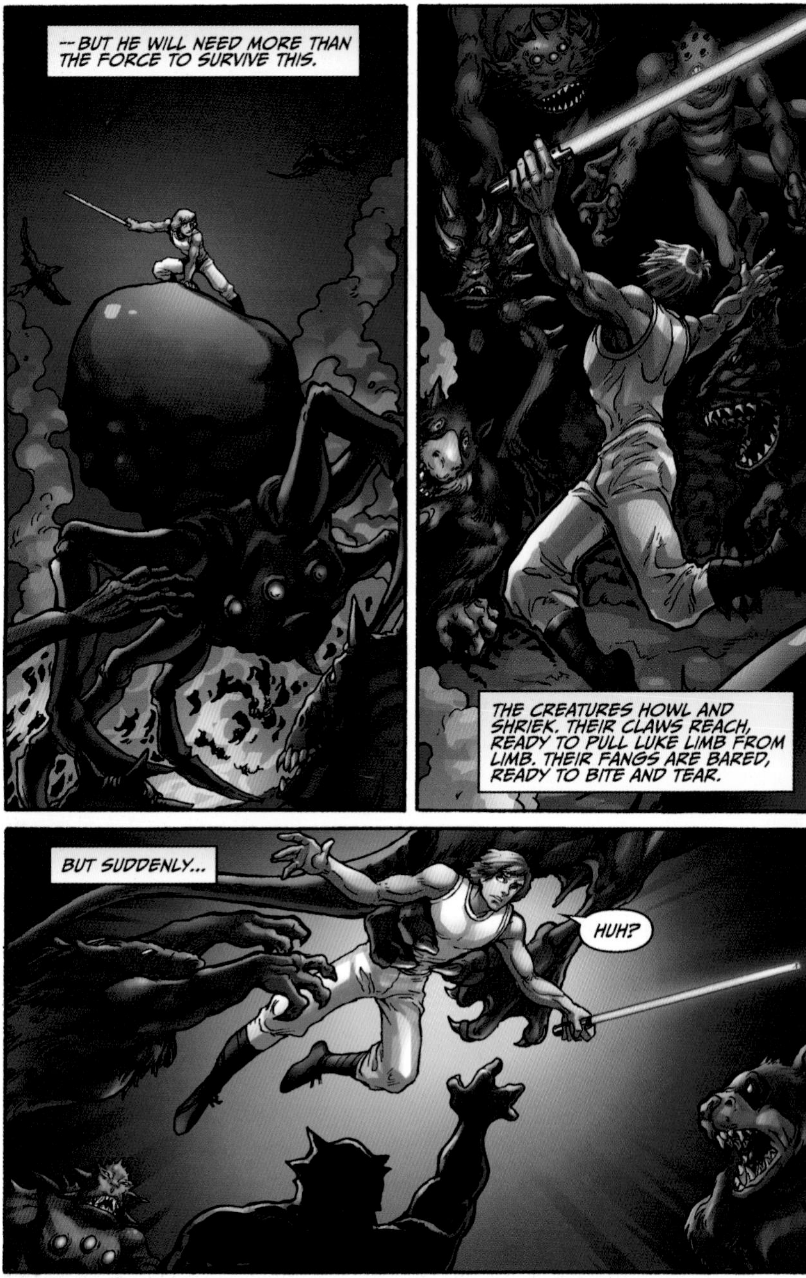
--BUT HE WILL NEED MORE THAN THE FORCE TO SURVIVE THIS.
THE CREATURES HOWL AND SHRIEK. THEIR CLAWS REACH, READY TO PULL LUKE LIMB FROM LIMB. THEIR FANGS ARE BARED, READY TO BITE AND TEAR.
BUT SUDDENLY...
HUH?

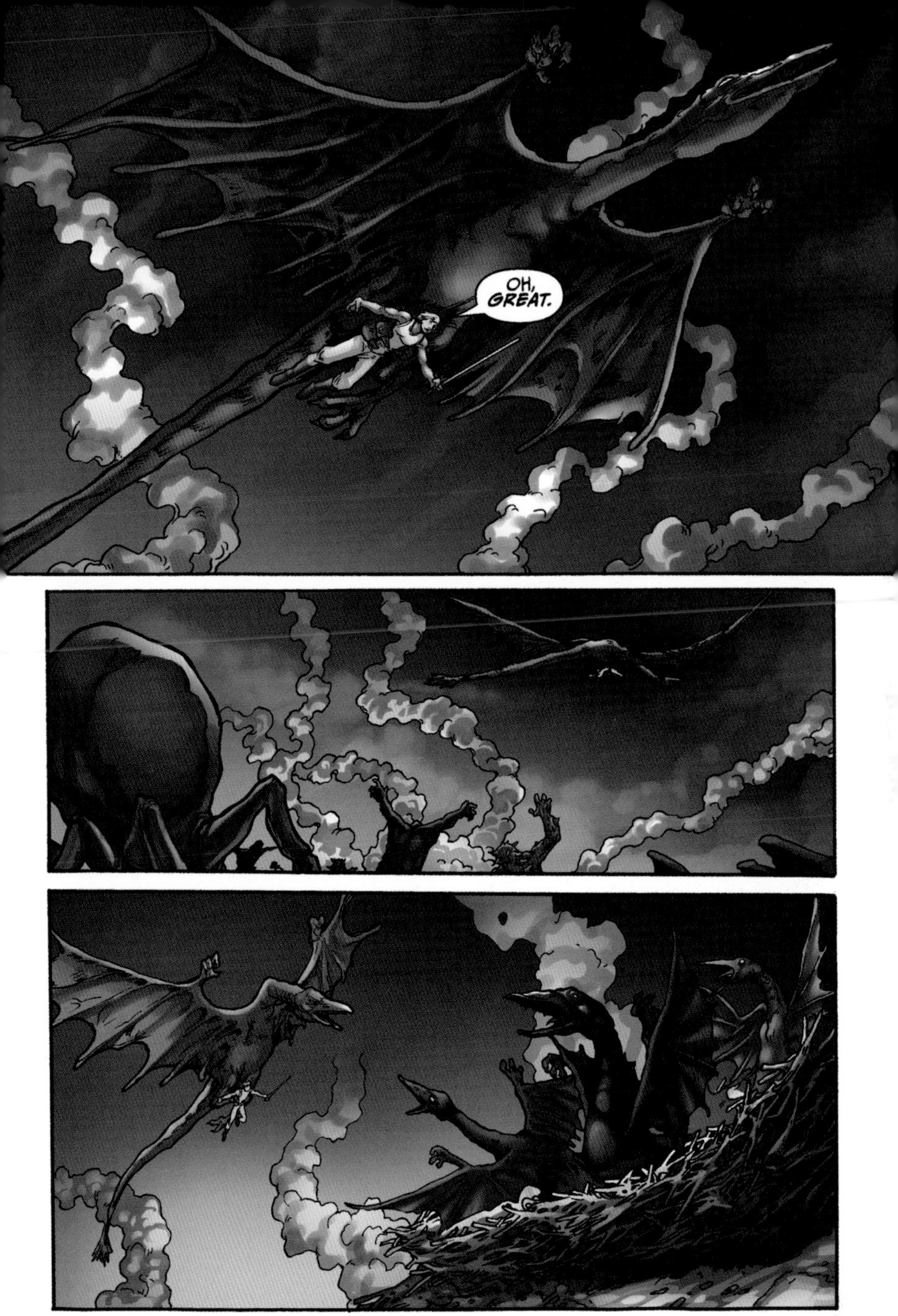
OH, GREAT.

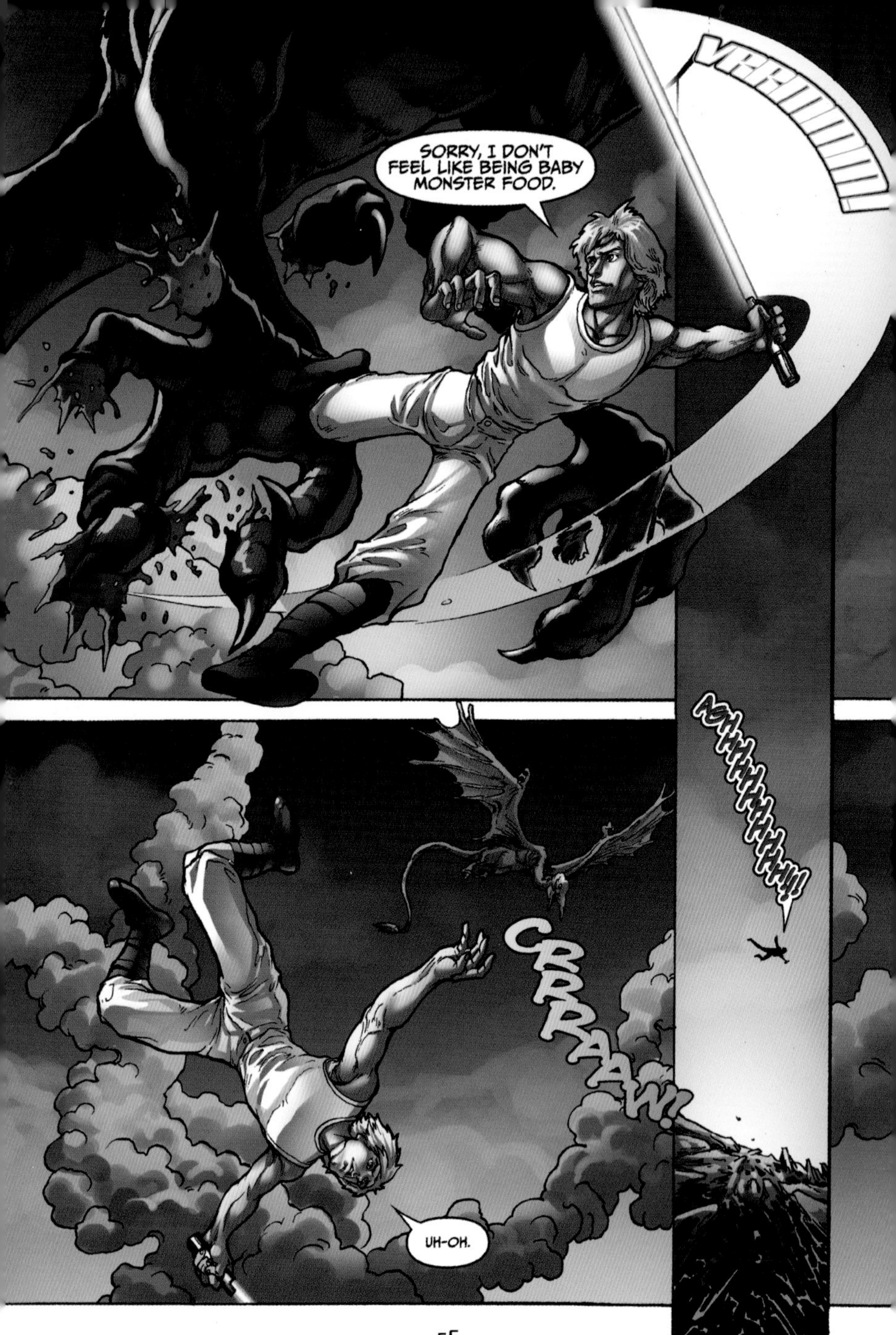
SORRY, I DON'T FEEL LIKE BEING BABY MONSTER FOOD.
VRRUUUUUM!
CRRAAAW!!
UH-OH.

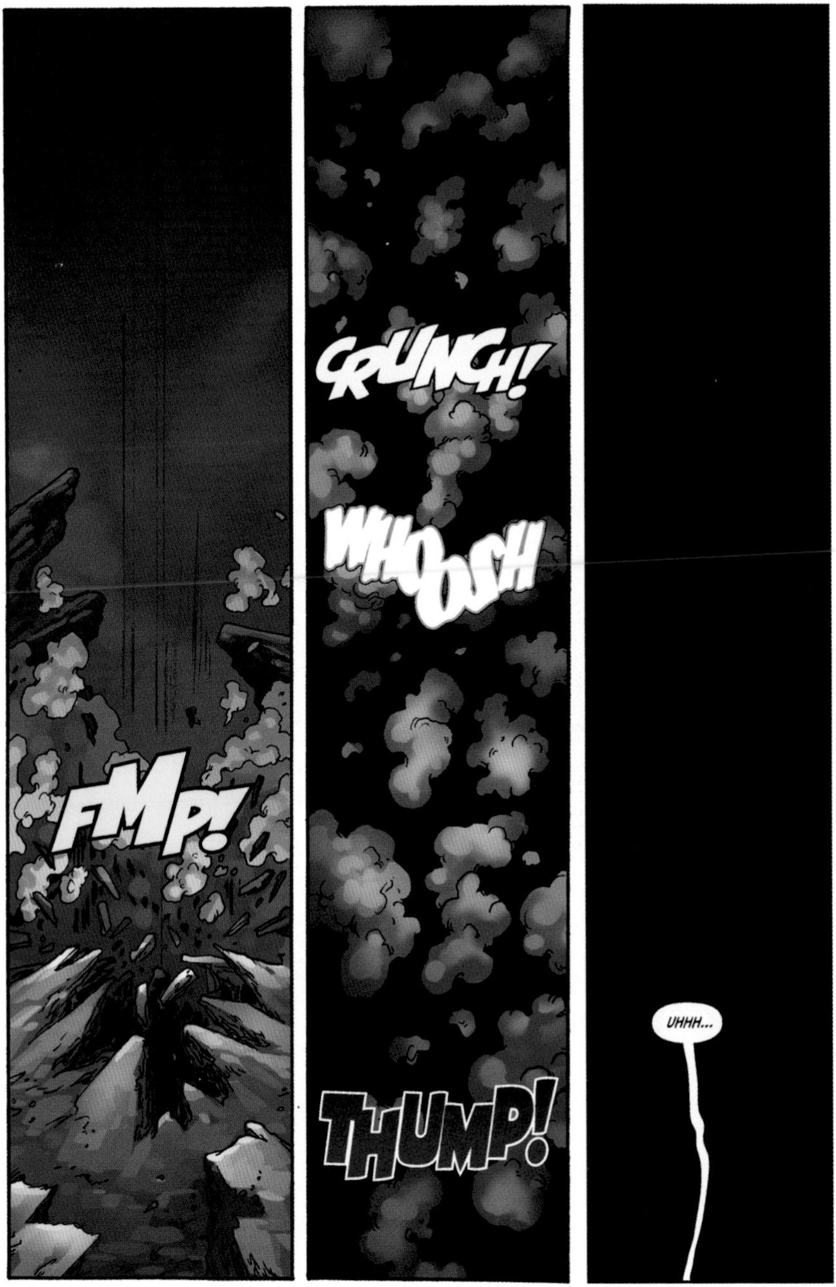
FMP!
CRUNCH!
WHOOOSH
THUMP!
UHHH...

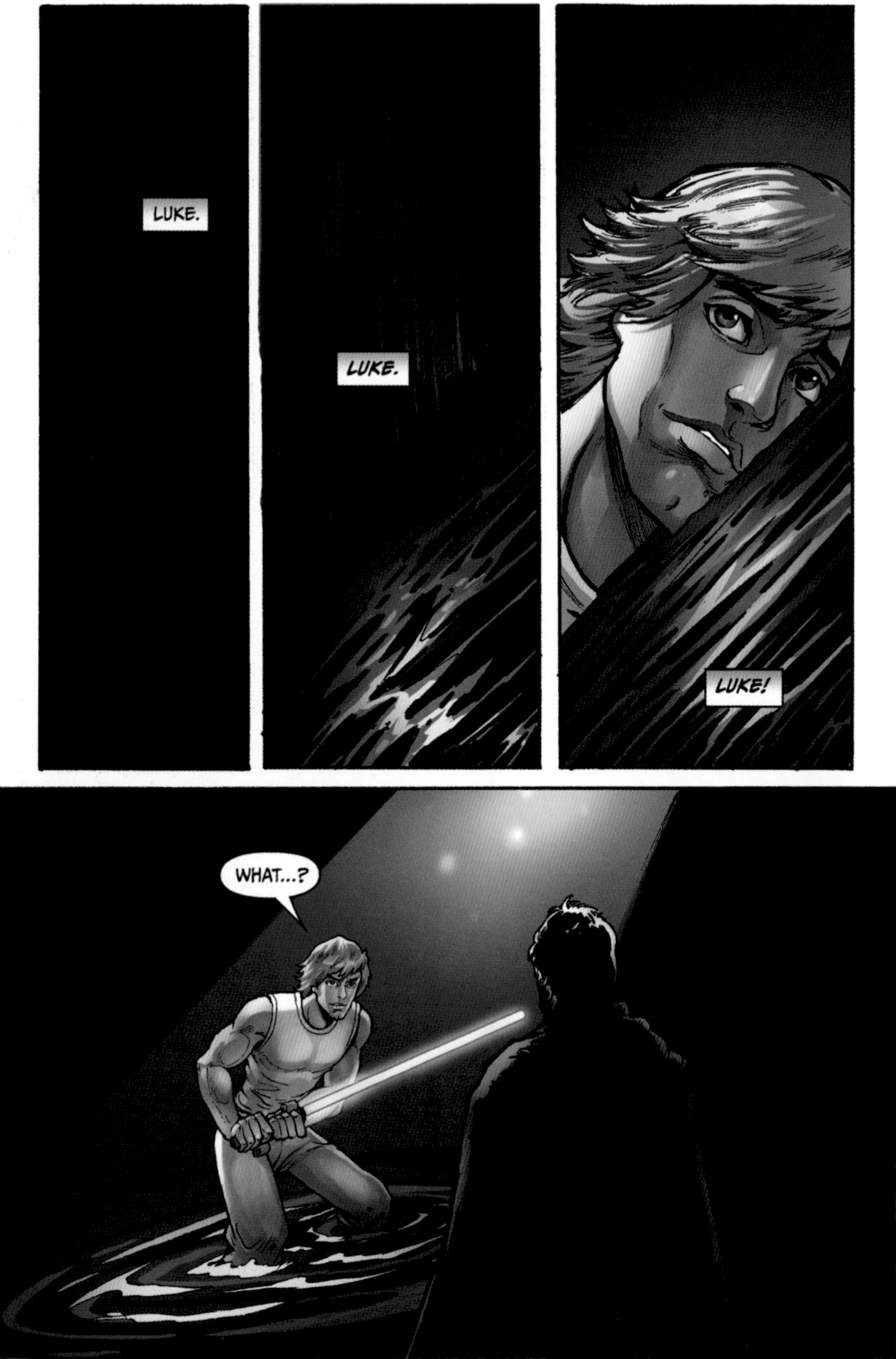
LUKE.
LUKE.
LUKE!
WHAT...?

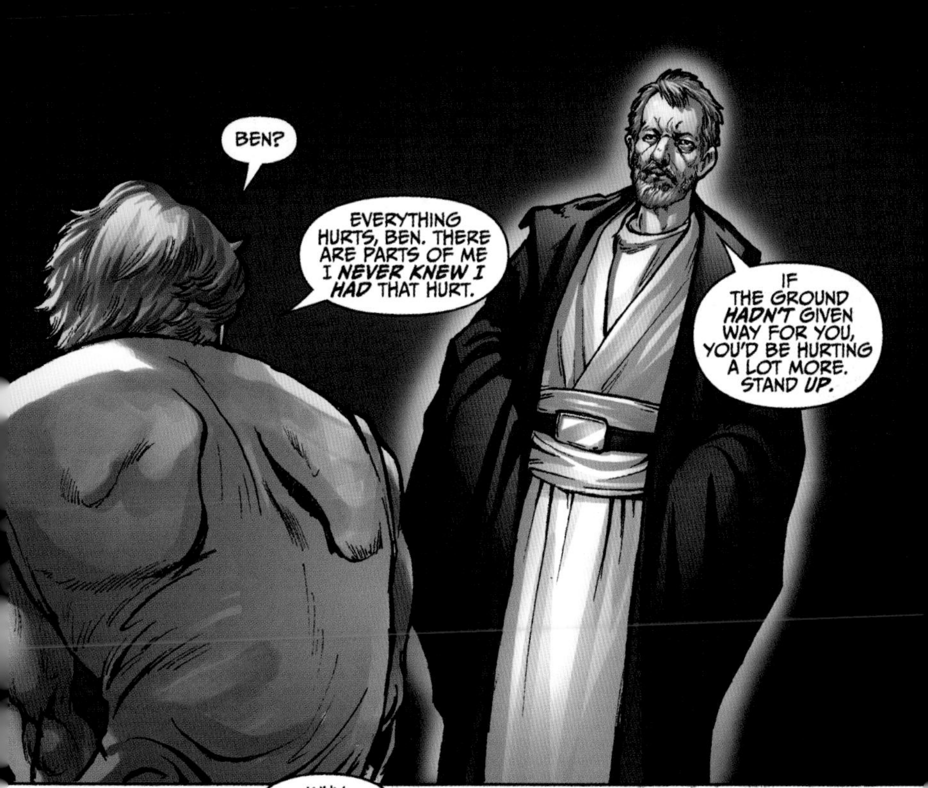
BEN?
EVERYTHING HURTS, BEN. THERE ARE PARTS OF ME I NEVER KNEW I HAD THAT HURT.
IF THE GROUND HADN'T GIVEN WAY FOR YOU, YOU'D BE HURTING A LOT MORE. STAND UP.

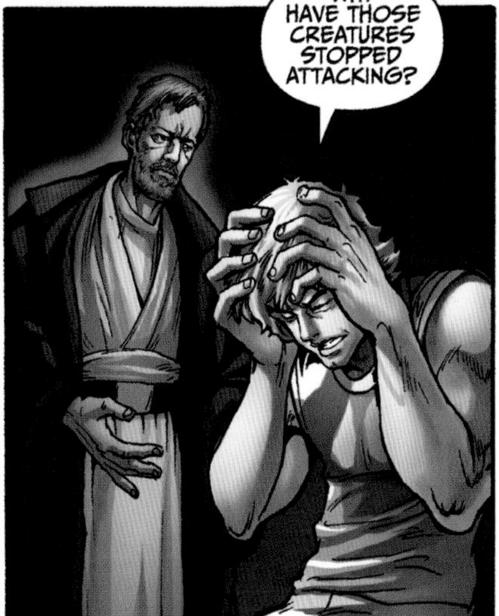
WHY HAVE THOSE CREATURES STOPPED ATTACKING?

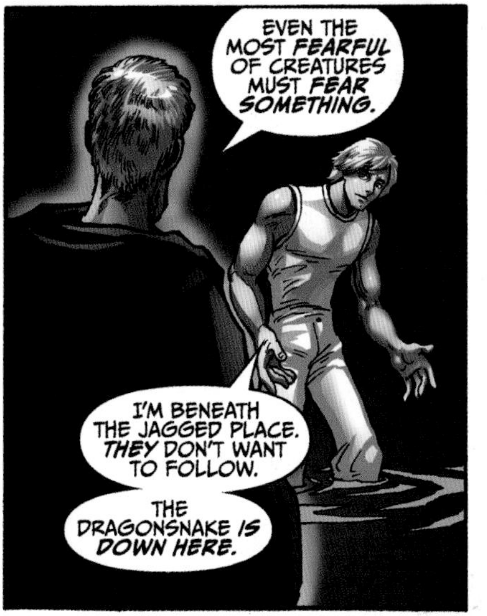
EVEN THE MOST FEARFUL OF CREATURES MUST FEAR SOMETHING.
I'M BENEATH THE JAGGED PLACE. THEY DON'T WANT TO FOLLOW.
THE DRAGONSNAKE IS DOWN HERE.

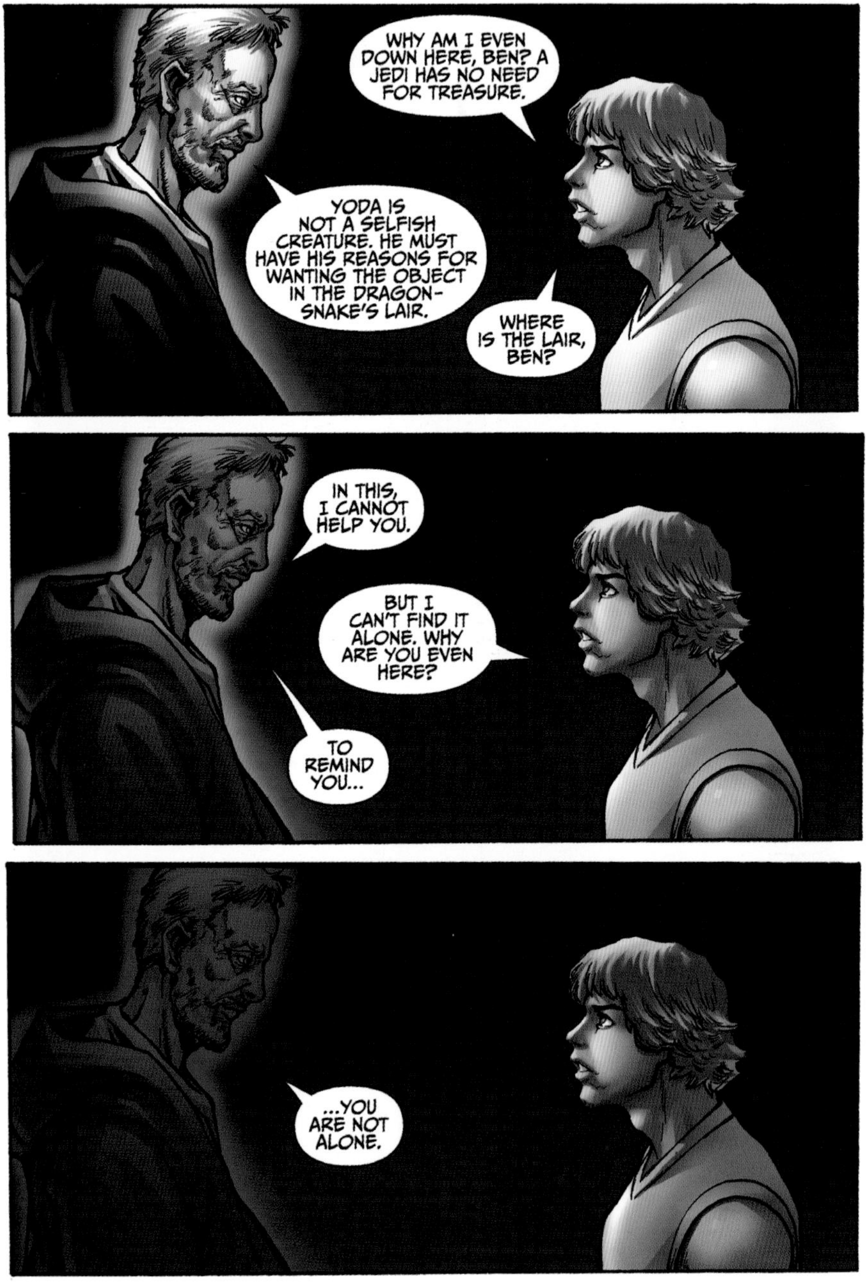
WHY AM I EVEN DOWN HERE, BEN? A JEDI HAS NO NEED FOR TREASURE.
YODA IS NOT A SELFISH CREATURE. HE MUST HAVE HIS REASONS FOR WANTING THE OBJECT IN THE DRAGON-SNAKE'S LAIR.
WHERE IS THE LAIR, BEN?
IN THIS, I CANNOT HELP YOU.
BUT I CAN'T FIND IT ALONE. WHY ARE YOU EVEN HERE?
TO REMIND YOU...
...YOU ARE NOT ALONE.

RIGHT. LIKE MASTER YODA SAID...

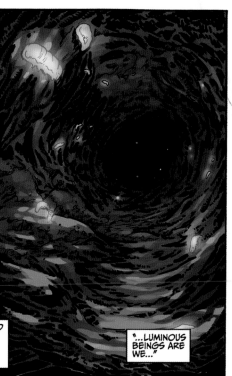

"...MY ALLY IS THE FORCE. AND A POWERFUL ALLY IT IS. LIFE CREATES IT, MAKES IT GROW. ITS ENERGY SURROUNDS US AND BINDS US..."

"...LUMINOUS BEINGS ARE WE..."

THERE IS A PLACE IN THESE TUNNELS WHERE THERE IS NO LIFE.

A PLACE OF DEATH.

THE DRAGONSNAKE'S LAIR.

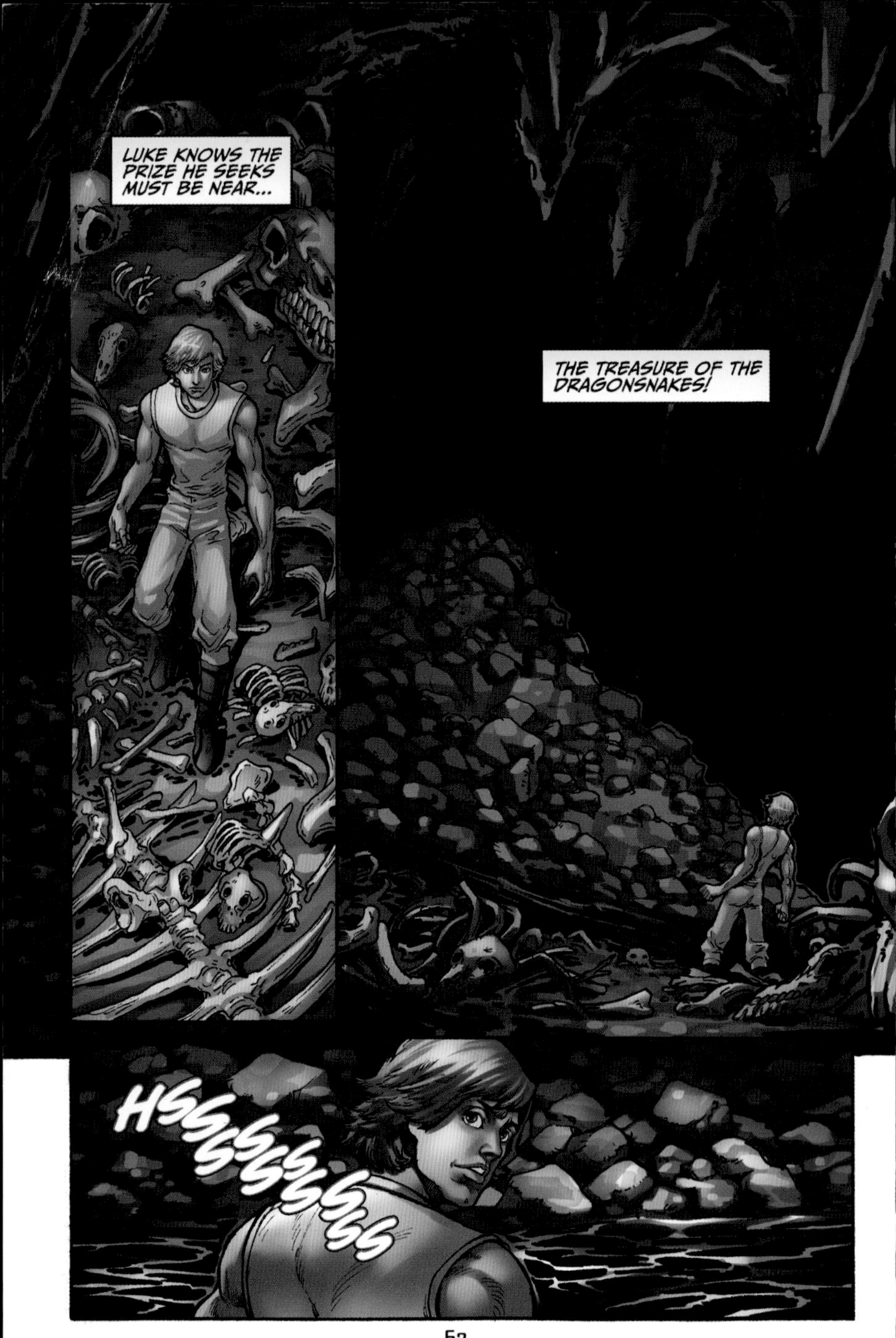
LUKE KNOWS THE PRIZE HE SEEKS MUST BE NEAR...
THE TREASURE OF THE DRAGONSNAKES!
HSSSSSSSSSS

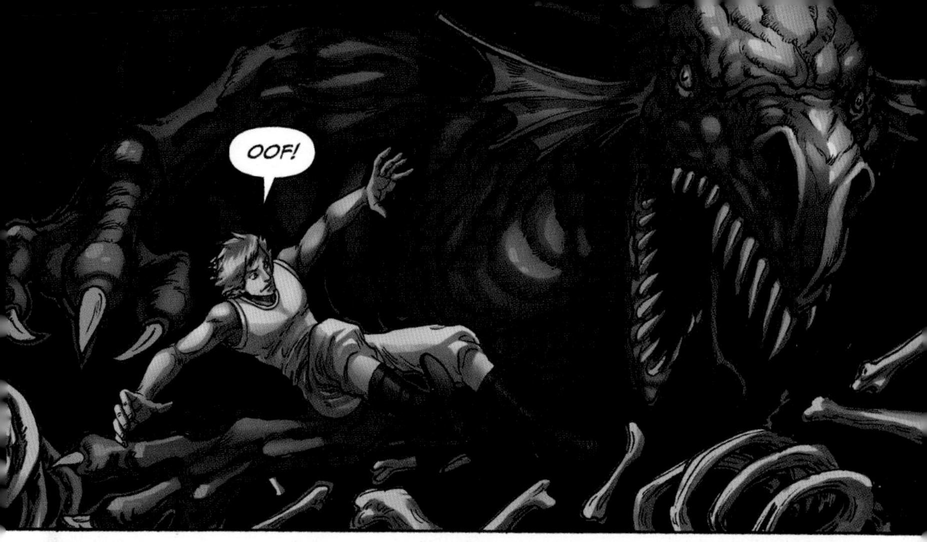
OOF!

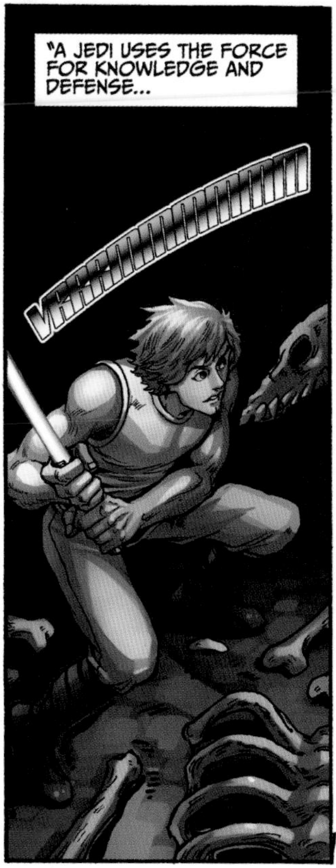
"A JEDI USES THE FORCE FOR KNOWLEDGE AND DEFENSE...

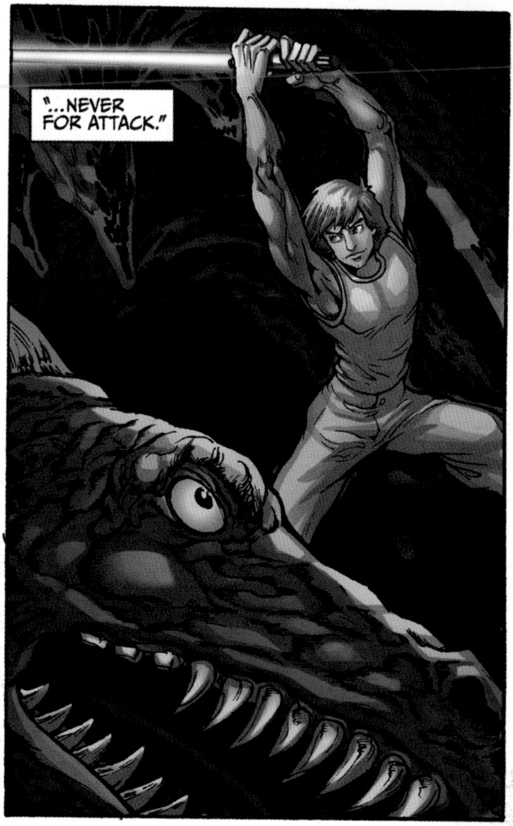
"...NEVER FOR ATTACK."

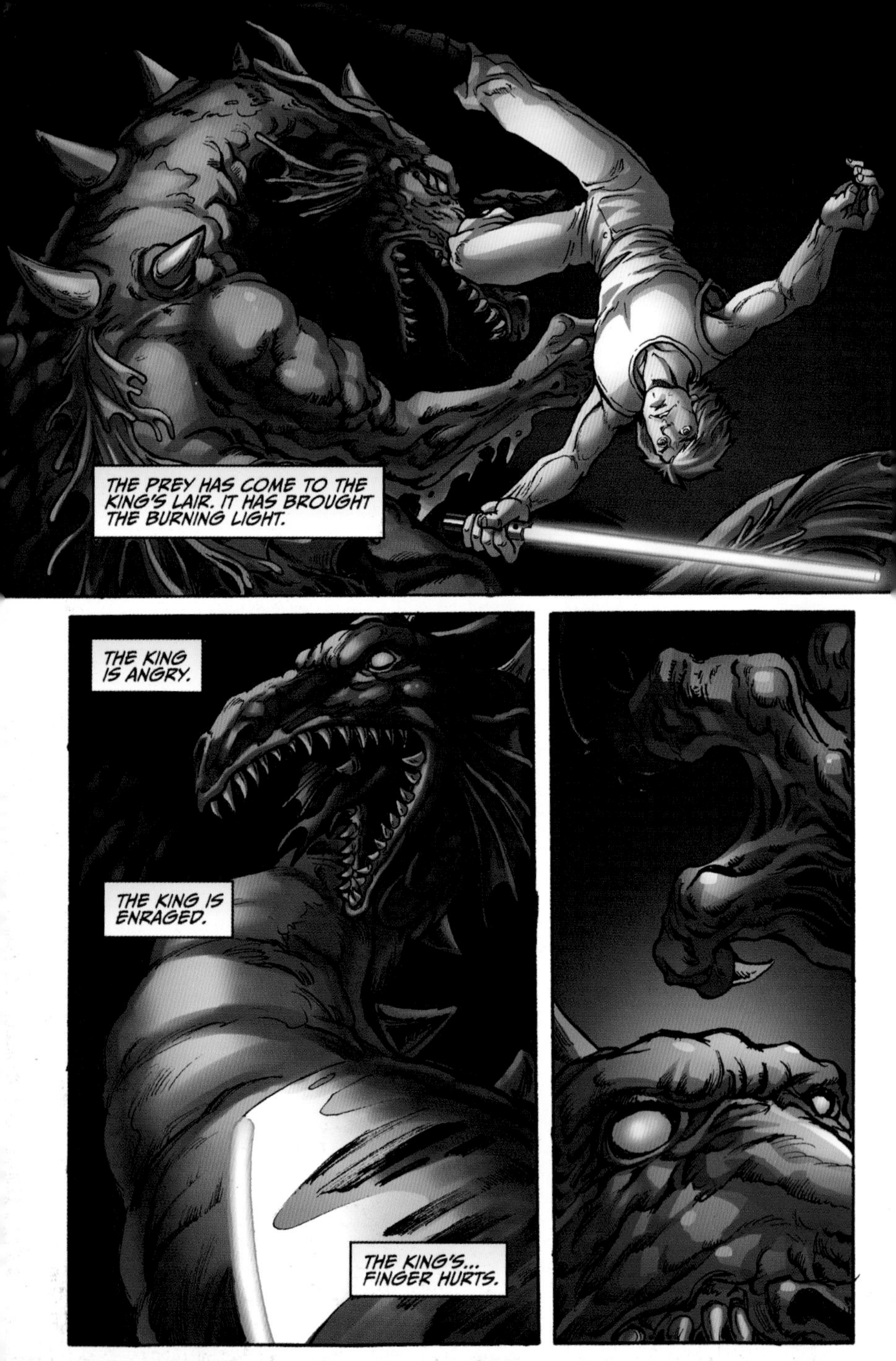
THE PREY HAS COME TO THE KING'S LAIR. IT HAS BROUGHT THE BURNING LIGHT.
THE KING IS ANGRY.
THE KING IS ENRAGED.
THE KING'S... FINGER HURTS.

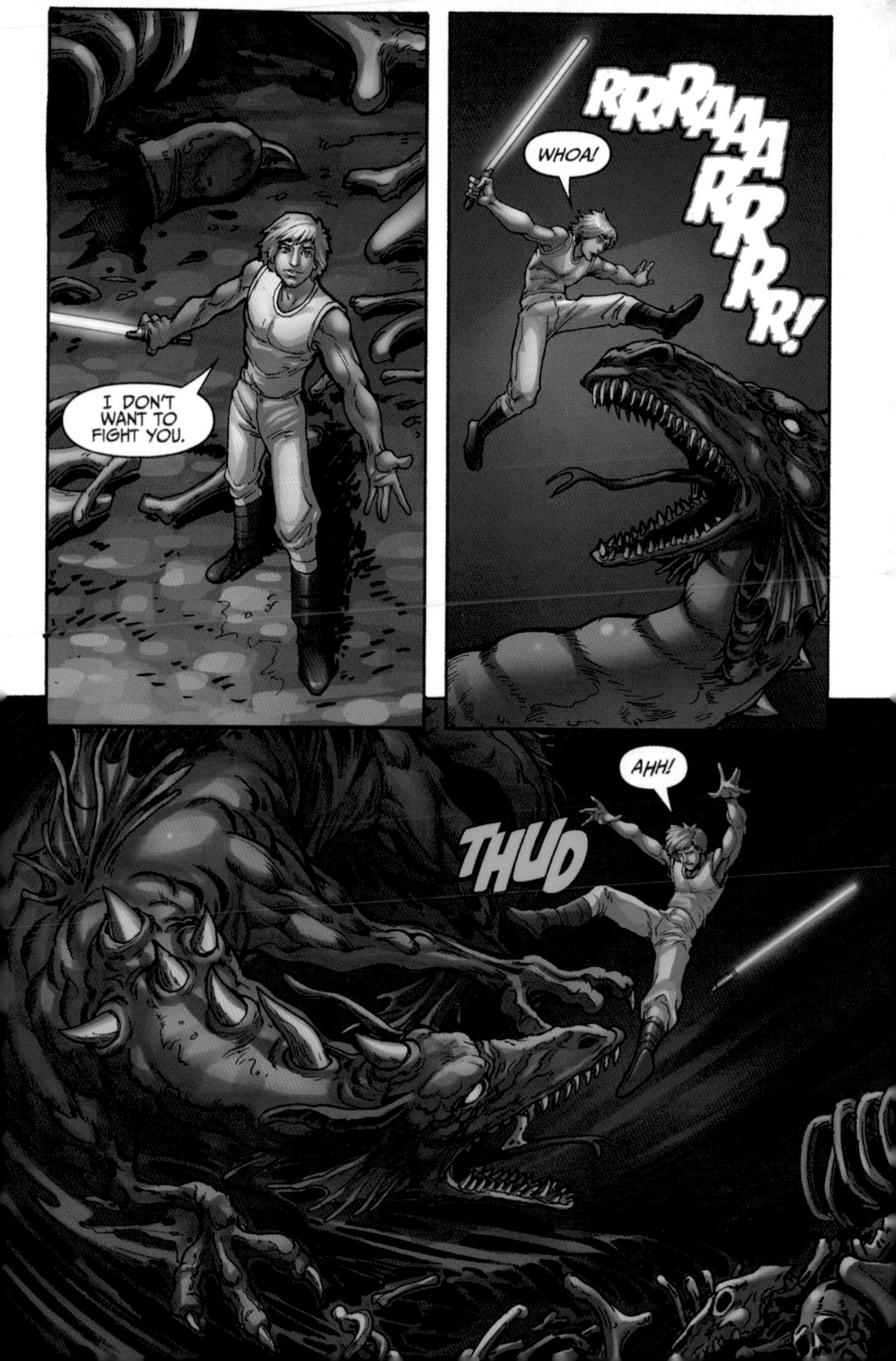
I DON'T WANT TO FIGHT YOU.
WHOA!
RRRRAAAARRRRR!
AHH!
THUD

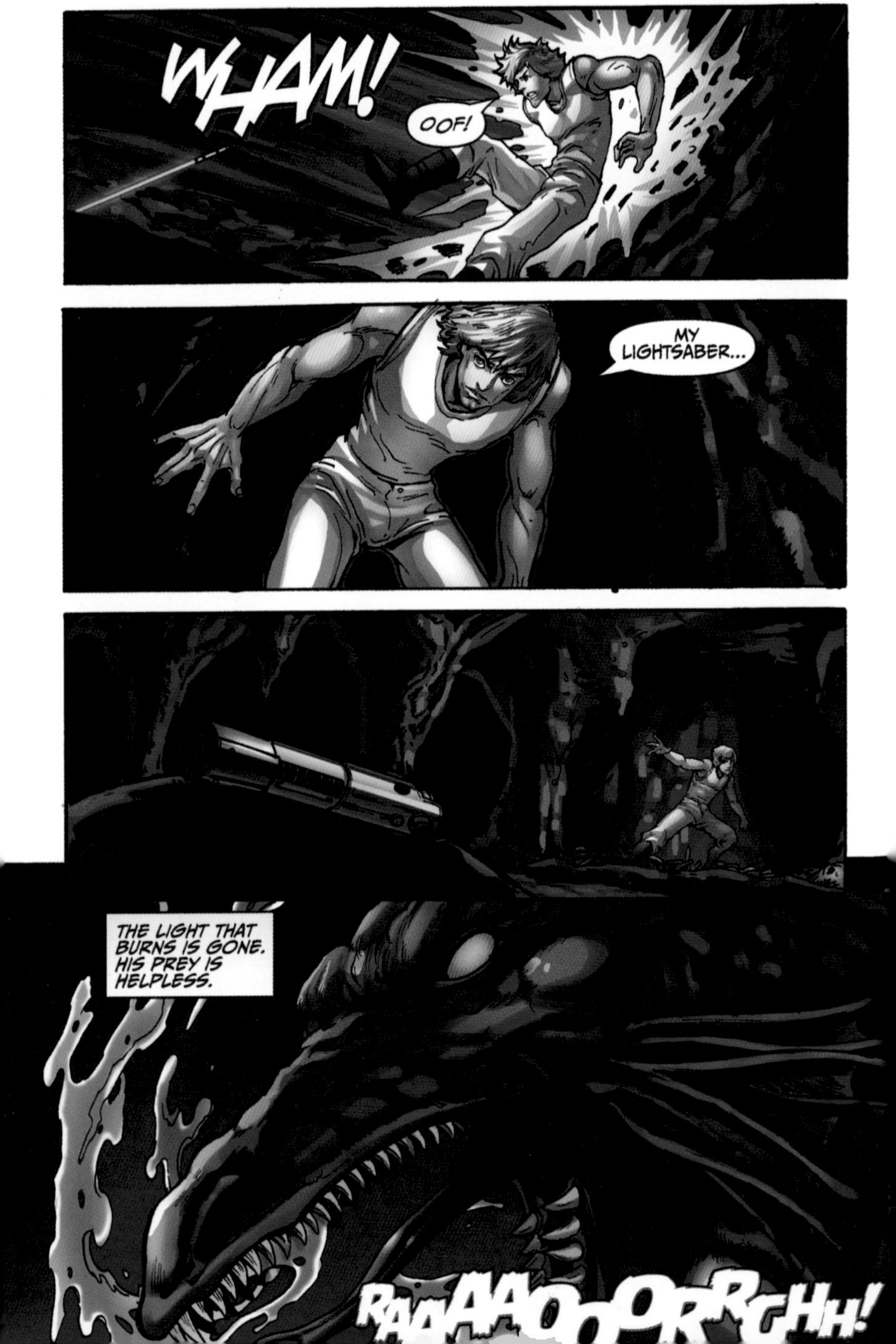
WHAM!
OOF!
MY LIGHTSABER...
THE LIGHT THAT BURNS IS GONE. HIS PREY IS HELPLESS.
RAAAAAOOOORRRGHH!

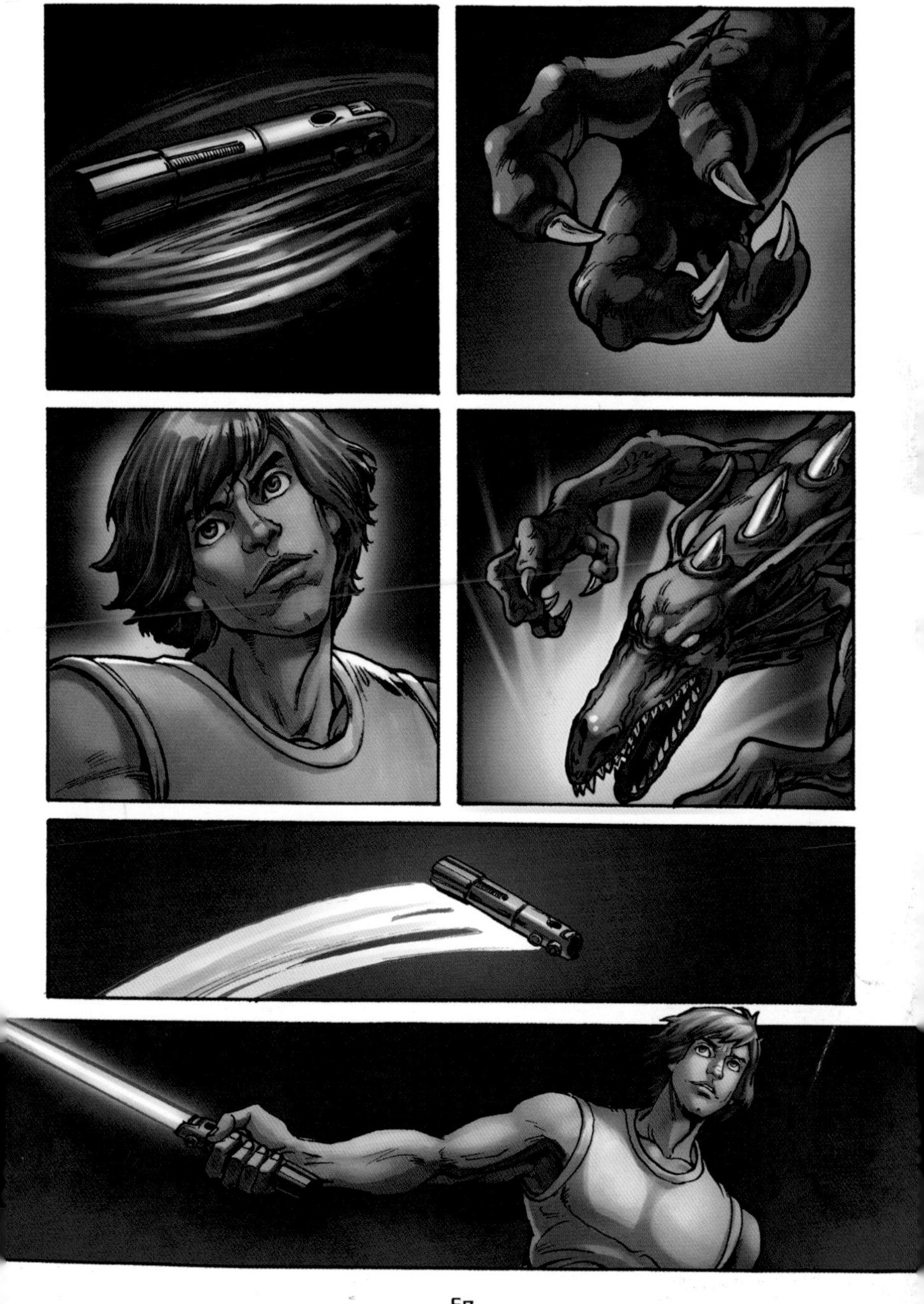

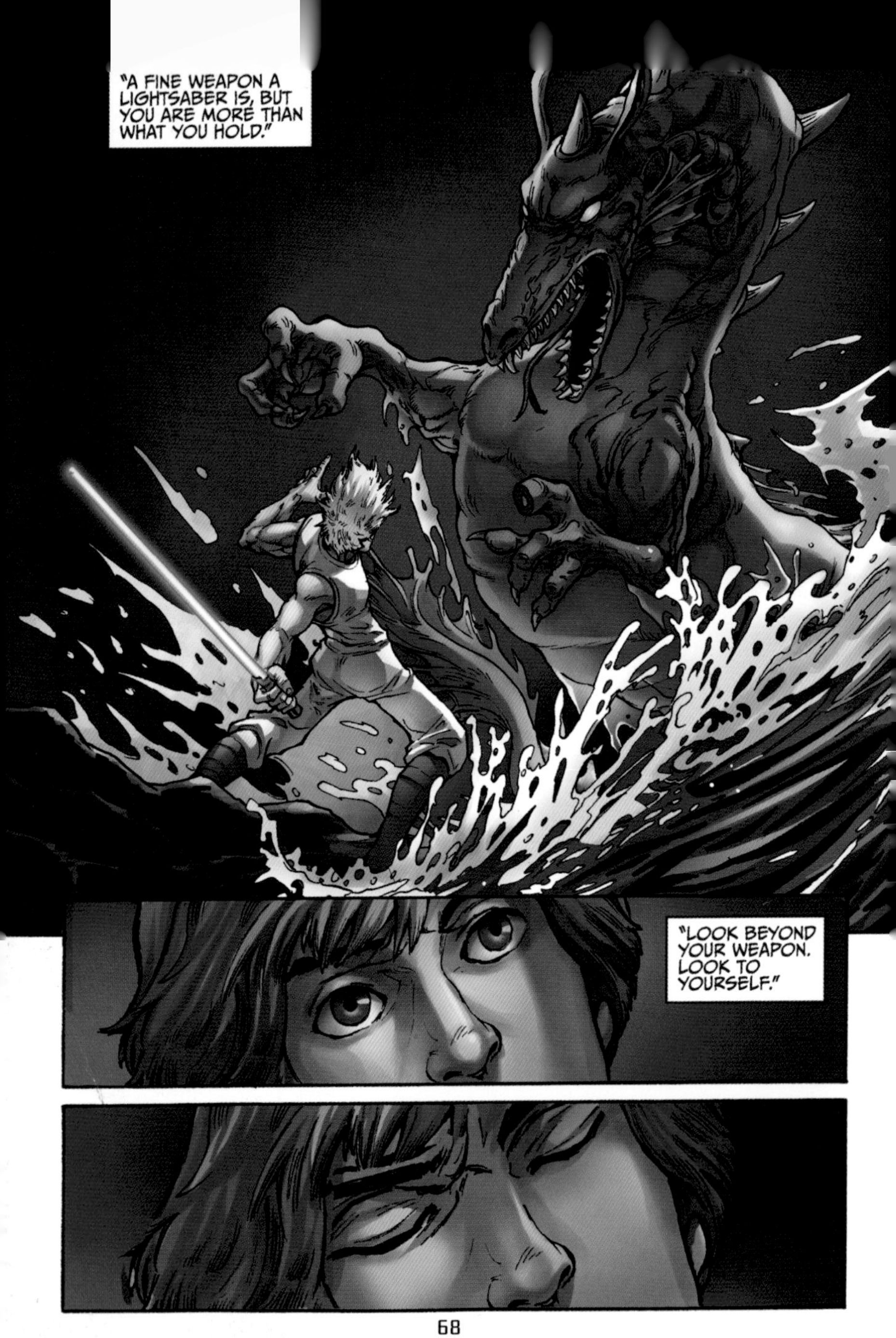
"A FINE WEAPON A LIGHTSABER IS, BUT YOU ARE MORE THAN WHAT YOU HOLD."
"LOOK BEYOND YOUR WEAPON. LOOK TO YOURSELF."

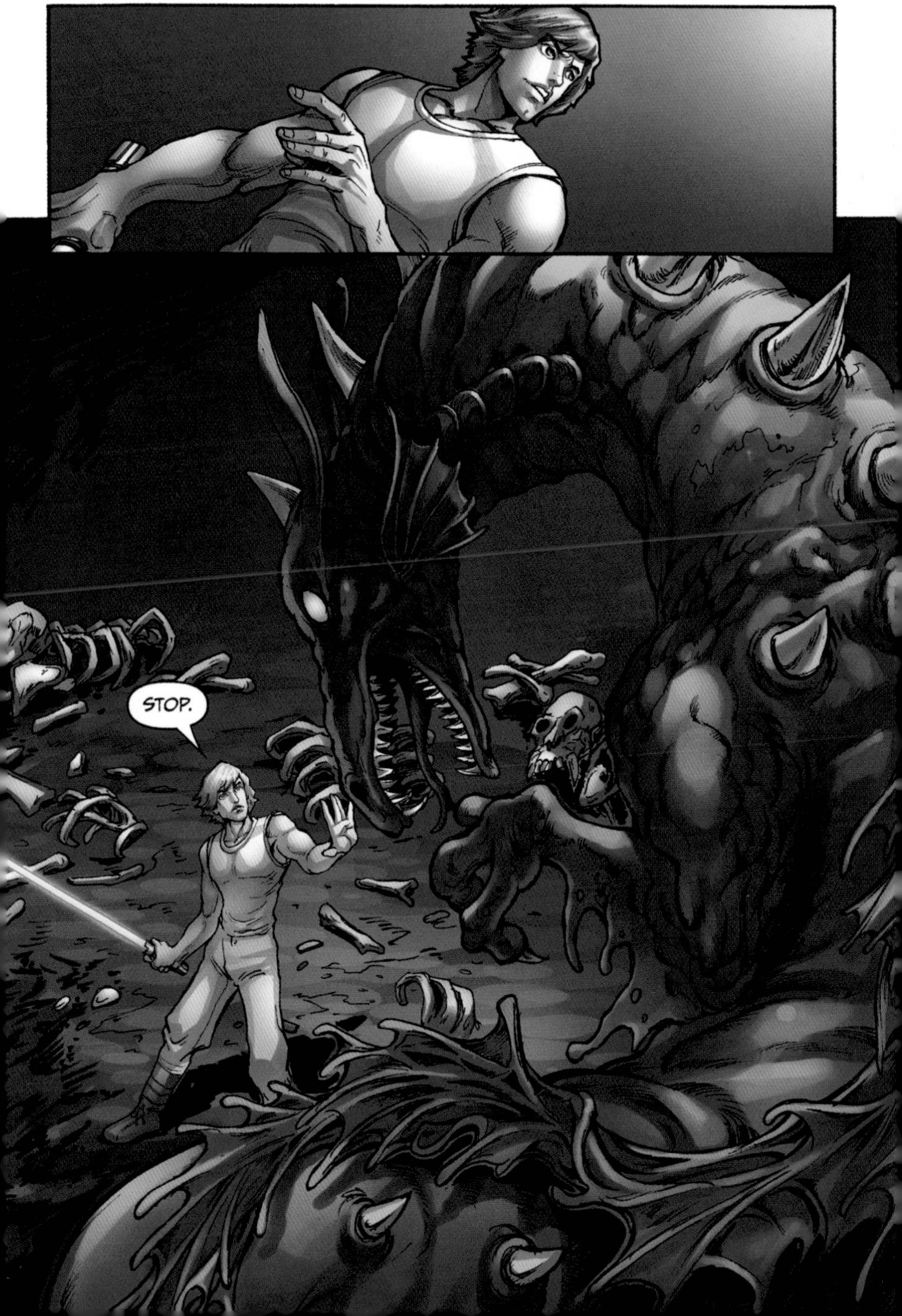
STOP.

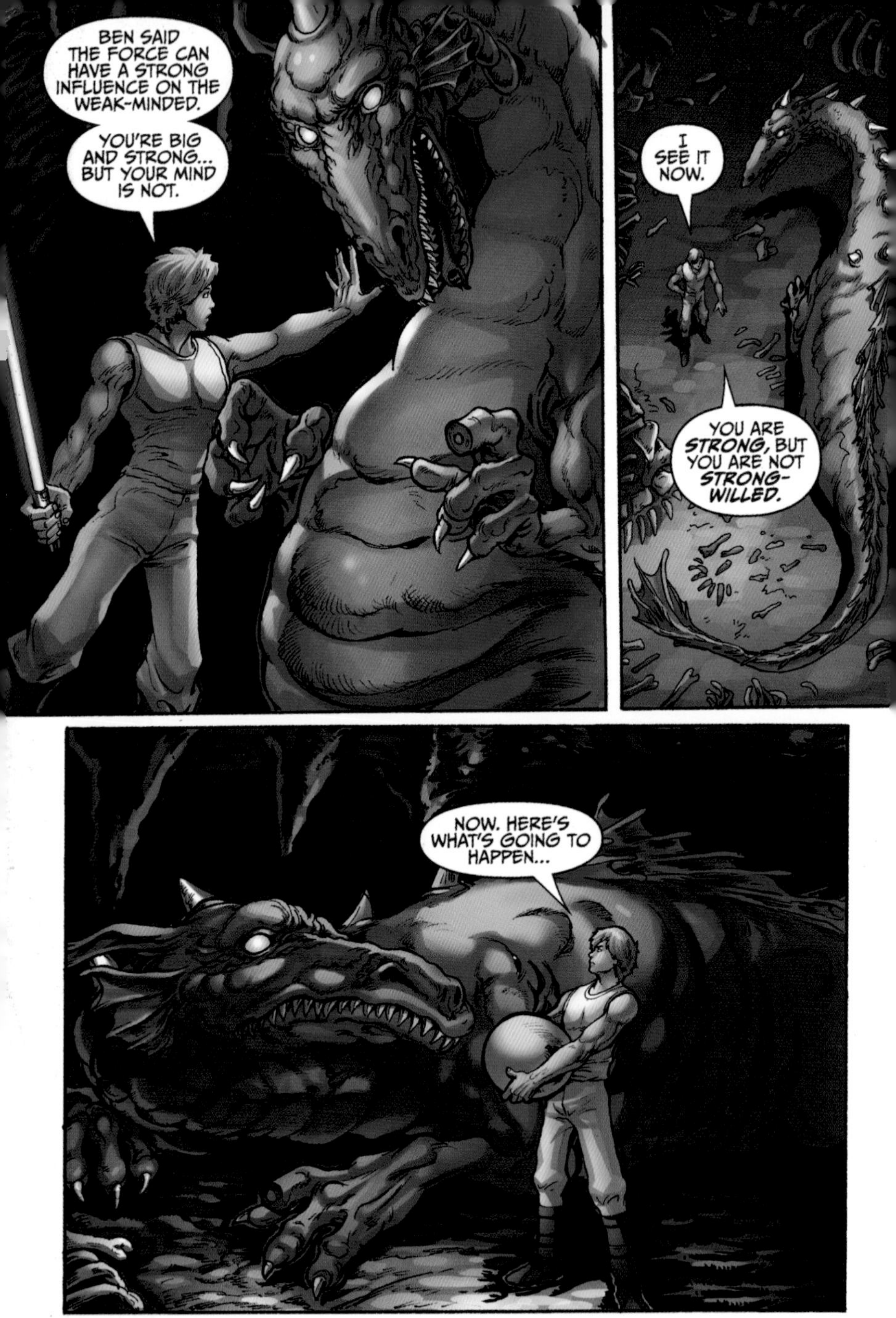
BEN SAID THE FORCE CAN HAVE A STRONG INFLUENCE ON THE WEAK-MINDED.
YOU'RE BIG AND STRONG... BUT YOUR MIND IS NOT.
I SEE IT NOW.
YOU ARE *STRONG*, BUT YOU ARE NOT *STRONG-WILLED.*
NOW. HERE'S WHAT'S GOING TO HAPPEN...

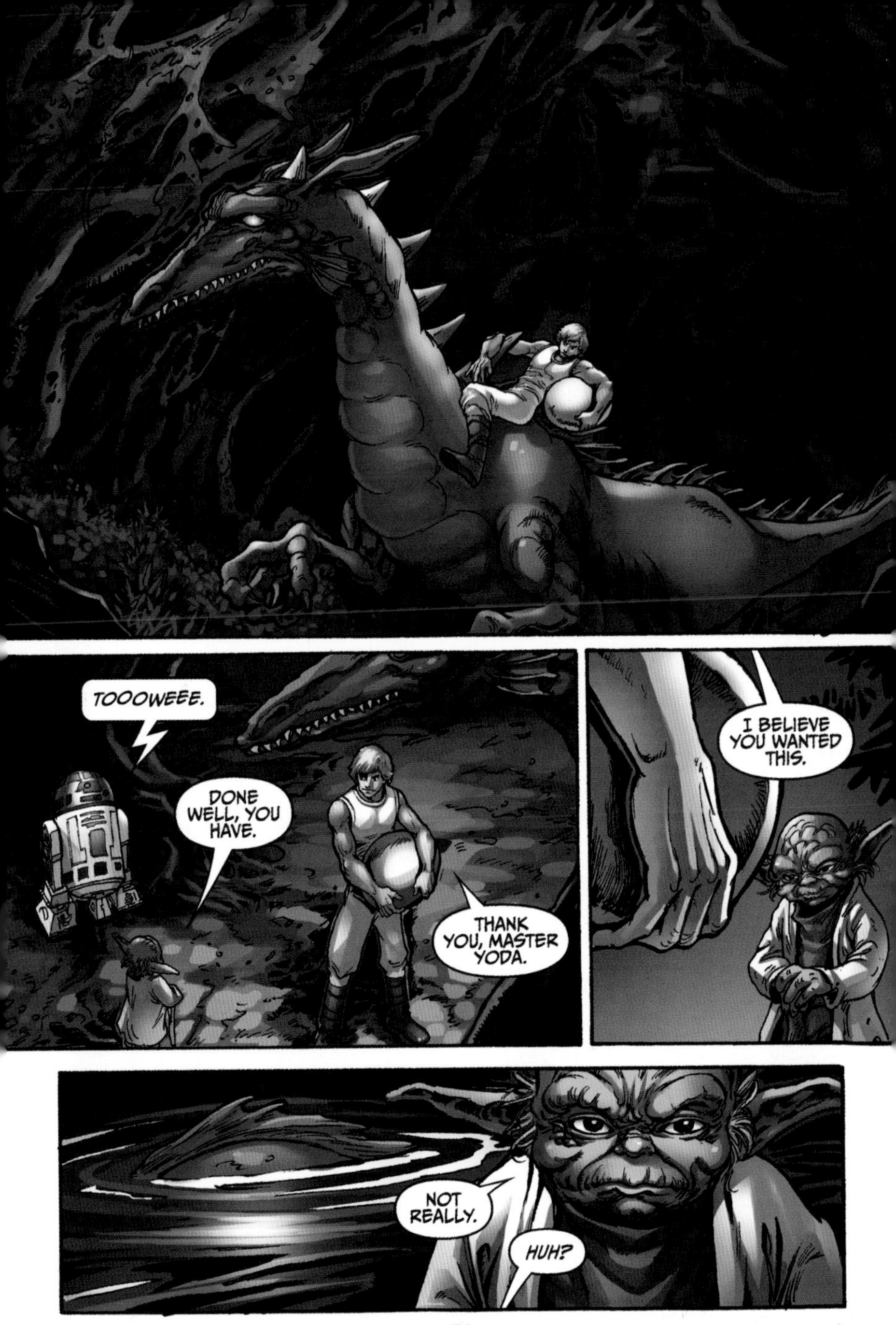
TOOOWEEE.
DONE WELL, YOU HAVE.
THANK YOU, MASTER YODA.
I BELIEVE YOU WANTED THIS.
NOT REALLY.
HUH?

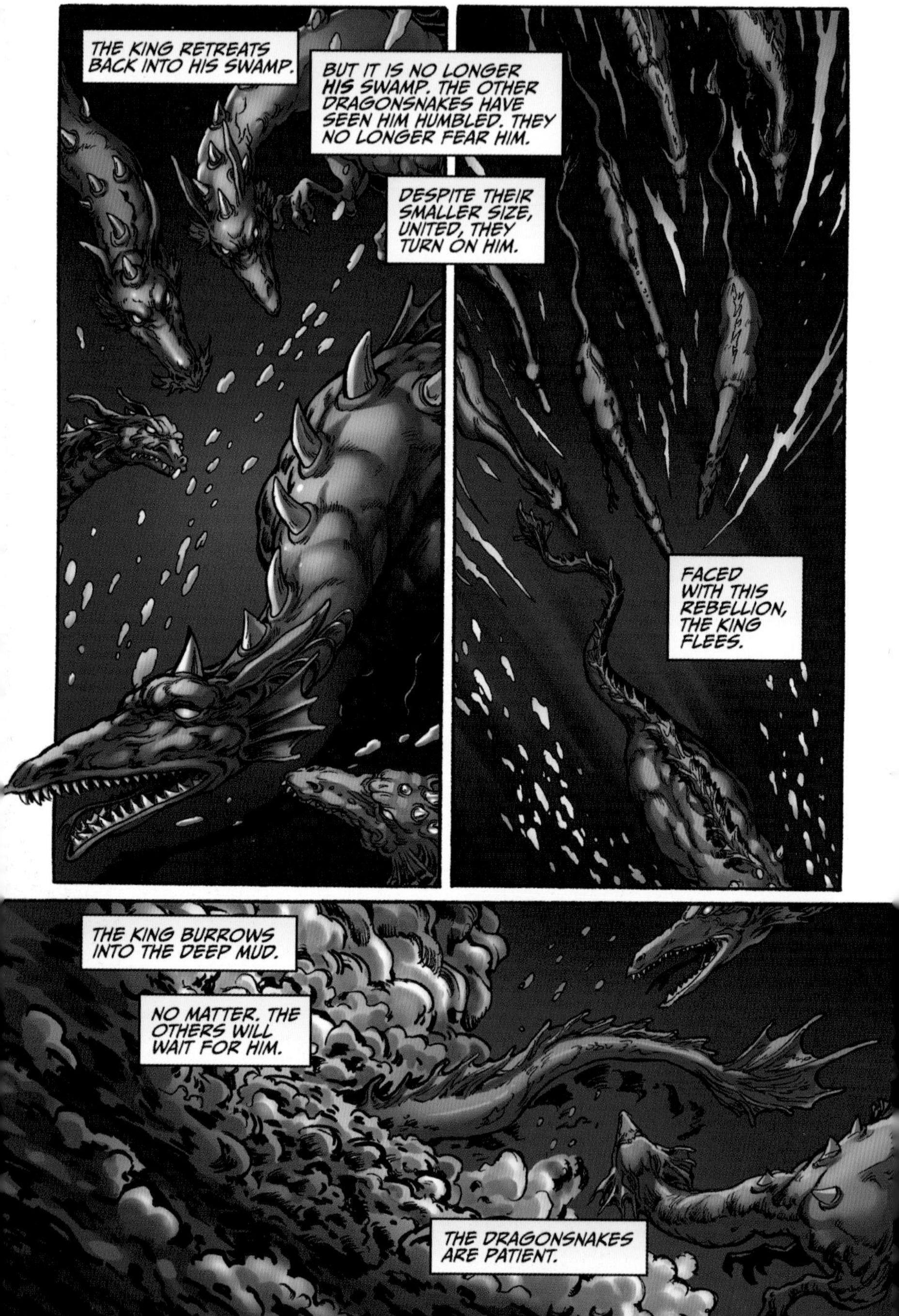
THE KING RETREATS BACK INTO HIS SWAMP.
BUT IT IS NO LONGER HIS SWAMP. THE OTHER DRAGONSNAKES HAVE SEEN HIM HUMBLED. THEY NO LONGER FEAR HIM.
DESPITE THEIR SMALLER SIZE, UNITED, THEY TURN ON HIM.
FACED WITH THIS REBELLION, THE KING FLEES.
THE KING BURROWS INTO THE DEEP MUD.
NO MATTER. THE OTHERS WILL WAIT FOR HIM.
THE DRAGONSNAKES ARE PATIENT.

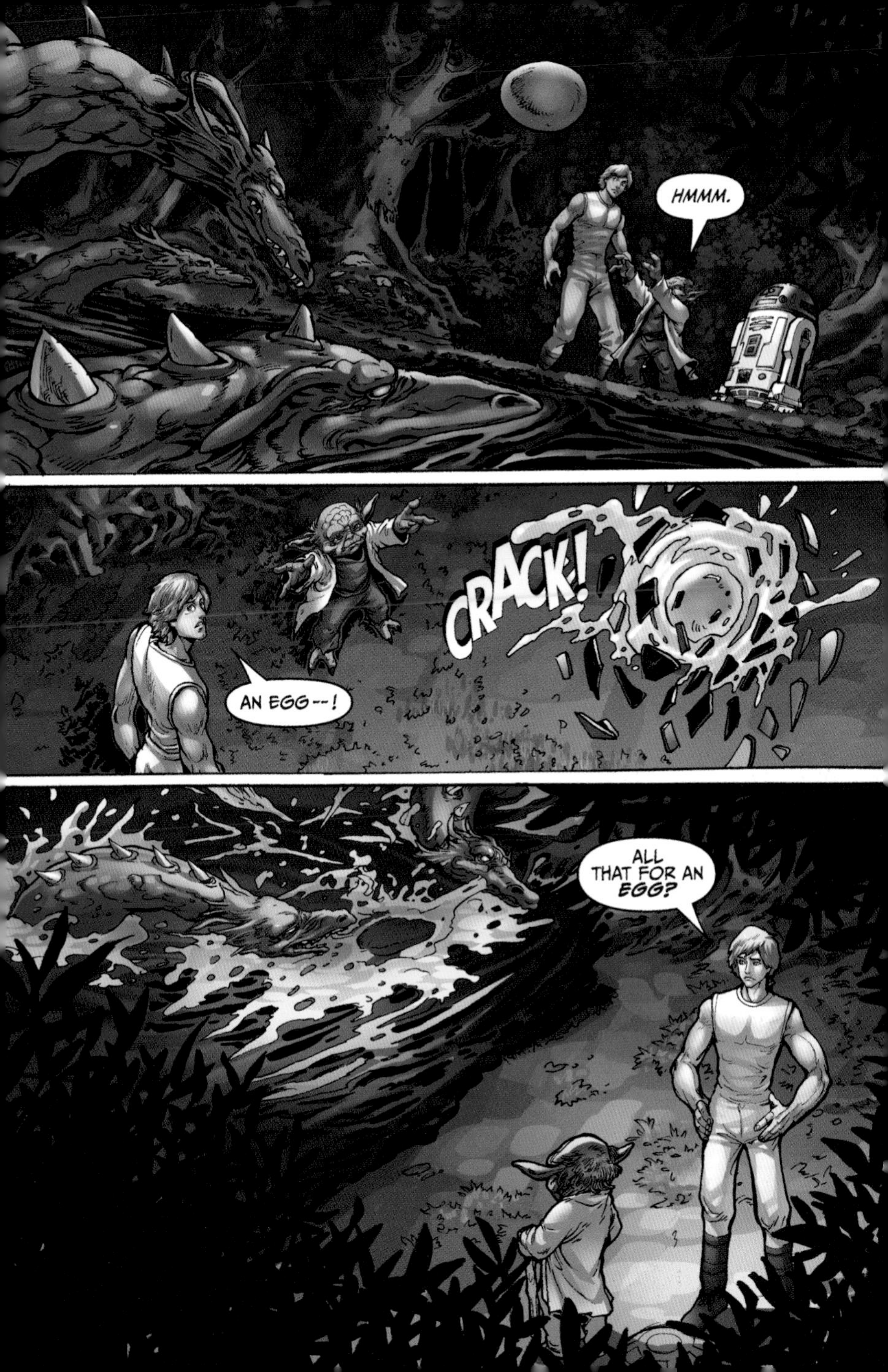
HMMM.
AN EGG--!
CRACK!
ALL THAT FOR AN EGG?

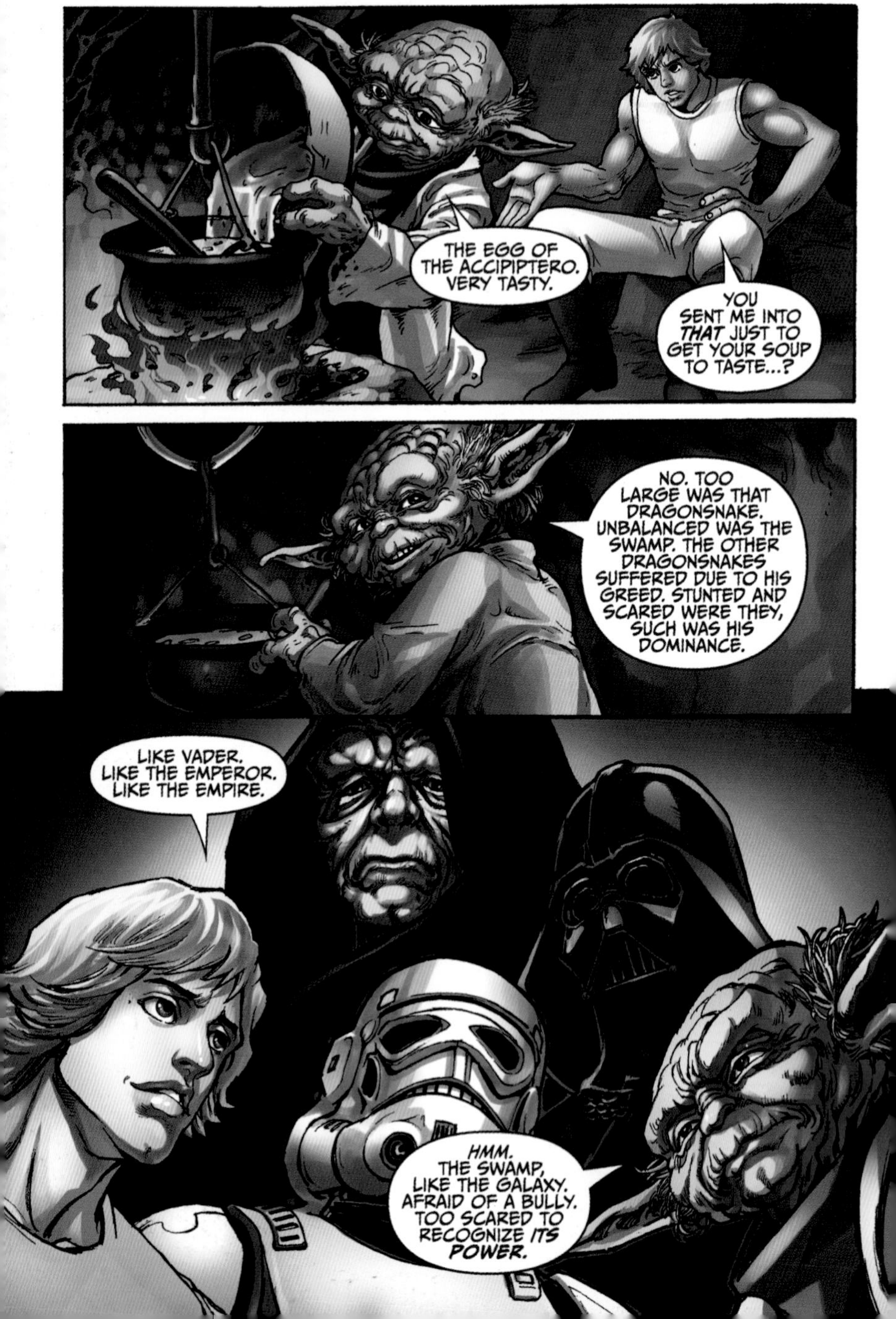
THE EGG OF THE ACCIPIPTERO. VERY TASTY.
YOU SENT ME INTO *THAT* JUST TO GET YOUR SOUP TO TASTE...?
NO. TOO LARGE WAS THAT DRAGONSNAKE. UNBALANCED WAS THE SWAMP. THE OTHER DRAGONSNAKES SUFFERED DUE TO HIS GREED. STUNTED AND SCARED WERE THEY, SUCH WAS HIS DOMINANCE.
LIKE VADER. LIKE THE EMPEROR. LIKE THE EMPIRE.
HMM. THE SWAMP, LIKE THE GALAXY. AFRAID OF A BULLY. TOO SCARED TO RECOGNIZE *ITS* *POWER.*

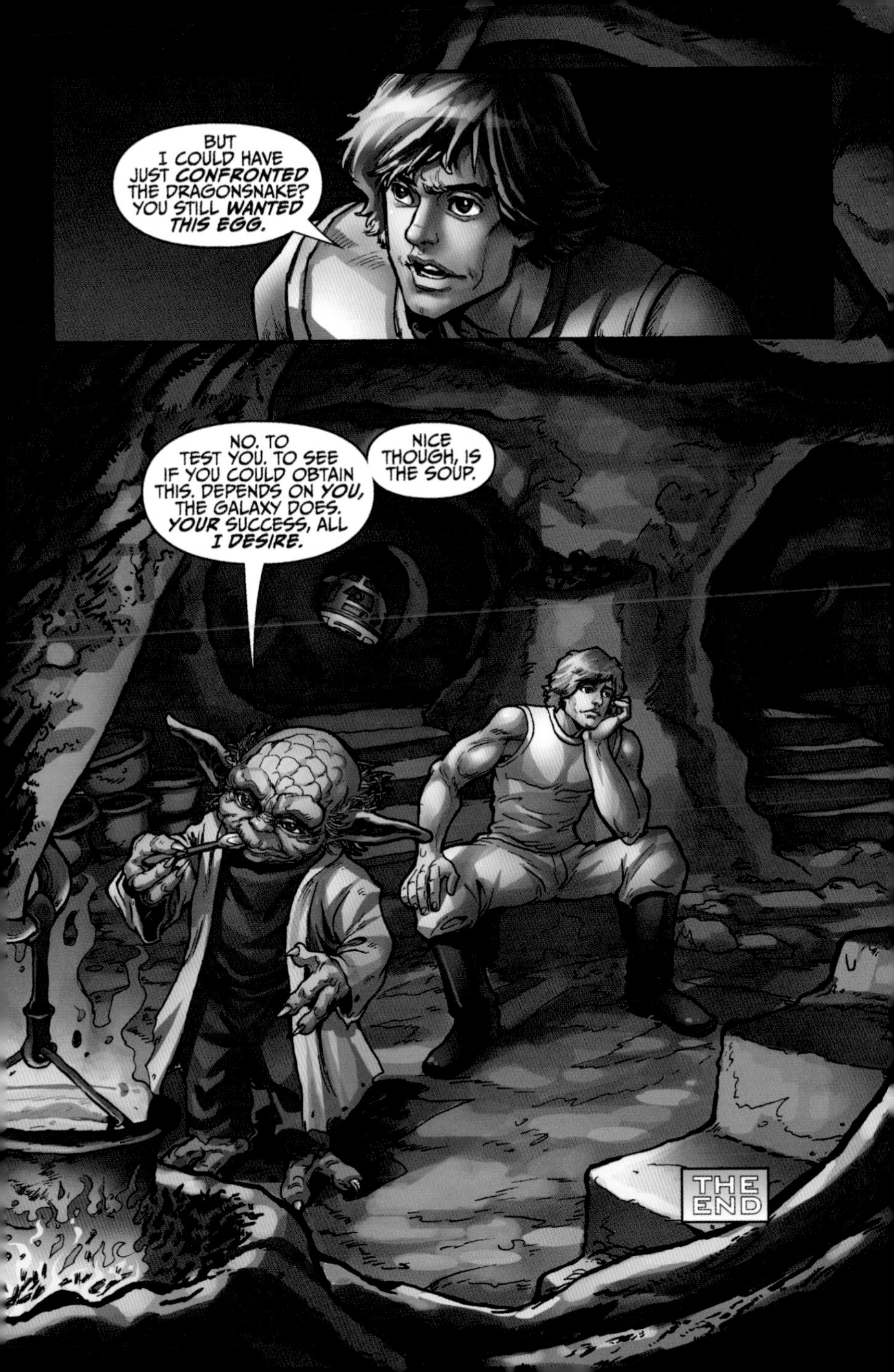
BUT I COULD HAVE JUST CONFRONTED THE DRAGONSNAKE? YOU STILL WANTED THIS EGG.
NO. TO TEST YOU. TO SEE IF YOU COULD OBTAIN THIS. DEPENDS ON YOU, THE GALAXY DOES. YOUR SUCCESS, ALL I DESIRE.
NICE THOUGH, IS THE SOUP.
THE END

President and Publisher **Mike Richardson**

Executive Vice President **Neil Hankerson**

Chief Financial Officer **Tom Weddle**

Vice President of Publishing **Randy Stradley**

Vice President of Business Development **Michael Martens**

Vice President of Marketing, Sales, and Licensing **Anita Nelson**

Vice President of Product Development **David Scroggy**

Vice President of Information Technology **Dale LaFountain**

Director of Purchasing **Darlene Vogel**

General Counsel **Ken Lizzi**

Editorial Director **Davey Estrada**

Senior Managing Editor **Scott Allie**

Senior Books Editor, Dark Horse Books **Chris Warner**

Executive Editor **Diana Schutz**

Director of Design and Production **Cary Grazzini**

Art Director **Lia Ribacchi**

Director of Scheduling **Cara Niece**

STAR WARS GRAPHIC NOVEL TIMELINE (IN YEARS)

Omnibus: Tales of the Jedi—5,000–3,986 BSW4
Knights of the Old Republic—3,964–3,963 BSW4
Jedi vs. Sith—1,000 BSW4
Omnibus: Rise of the Sith—33 BSW4
Episode I: The Phantom Menace—32 BSW4
Omnibus: Emissaries and Assassins—32 BSW4
Twilight—31 BSW4
Bounty Hunters—31 BSW4
The Hunt for Aurra Sing—30 BSW4
Darkness—30 BSW4
The Stark Hyperspace War—30 BSW4
Rite of Passage—28 BSW4
Jango Fett—27 BSW4
Zam Wesell—27 BSW4
Honor and Duty—24 BSW4
Episode II: Attack of the Clones—22 BSW4
Clone Wars—22–19 BSW4
Clone Wars Adventures—22–19 BSW4
General Grievous—22–19 BSW4
Episode III: Revenge of the Sith—19 BSW4
Dark Times—19 BSW4
Omnibus: Droids—5.5 BSW4
Boba Fett: Enemy of the Empire—3 BSW4
Underworld—1 BSW4
Episode IV: A New Hope—SW4
Classic Star Wars—0–3 ASW4
A Long Time Ago . . .—0–4 ASW4
Empire—0 ASW4
Rebellion—0 ASW4
Boba Fett: Man with a Mission—0 ASW4
Omnibus: Early Victories—0–3 ASW4
Jabba the Hutt: The Art of the Deal—1 ASW4
Episode V: The Empire Strikes Back—3 ASW4
Shadows of the Empire—3.5 ASW4
Episode VI: Return of the Jedi—4 ASW4
Mara Jade: By the Emperor's Hand—4 ASW4
Omnibus: X-Wing Rogue Squadron—4–5 ASW4
Heir to the Empire—9 ASW4
Dark Force Rising—9 ASW4
The Last Command—9 ASW4
Dark Empire—10 ASW4
Boba Fett: Death, Lies, and Treachery—10 ASW4
Crimson Empire—11 ASW4
Jedi Academy: Leviathan—12 ASW4
Union—19 ASW4
Chewbacca—25 ASW4
Legacy—130–137 ASW4

Old Republic Era
25,000 – 1000 years before
Star Wars: A New Hope

Rise of the Empire Era
1000 – 0 years before
Star Wars: A New Hope

Rebellion Era
0 – 5 years after
Star Wars: A New Hope

New Republic Era
5 – 25 years after
Star Wars: A New Hope

New Jedi Order Era
25+ years after
Star Wars: A New Hope

Legacy Era
130+ years after
Star Wars: A New Hope

Infinities
Does not apply to timeline

Sergio Aragonés Stomps Star Wars
Star Wars Tales
Star Wars Infinities
Tag and Bink
Star Wars Visionaries

BSW4 = before *Episode IV: A New Hope.* ASW4 = after *Episode IV: A New Hope.*

READY TO TRY SOME OTHER GREAT STAR WARS TITLES?

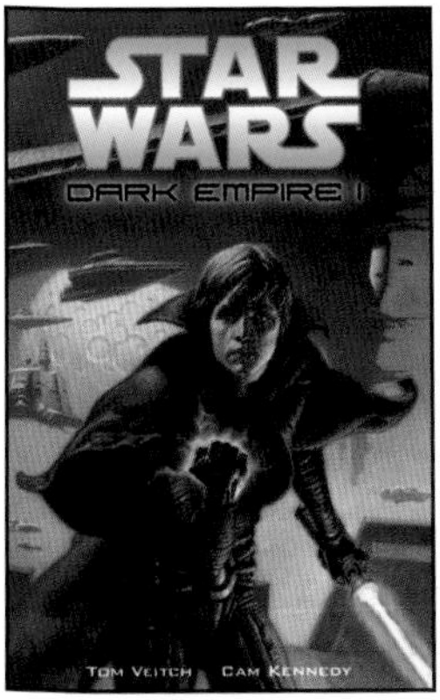
STAR WARS
DARK EMPIRE I
TOM VEITCH CAM KENNEDY

DARK EMPIRE

Join Luke, Leia, Han, and Chewie as they battle the Empire's latest super weapons: the gigantic, planet-destroying World Devastators!

ISBN 978-1-59307-039-7 | $16.99

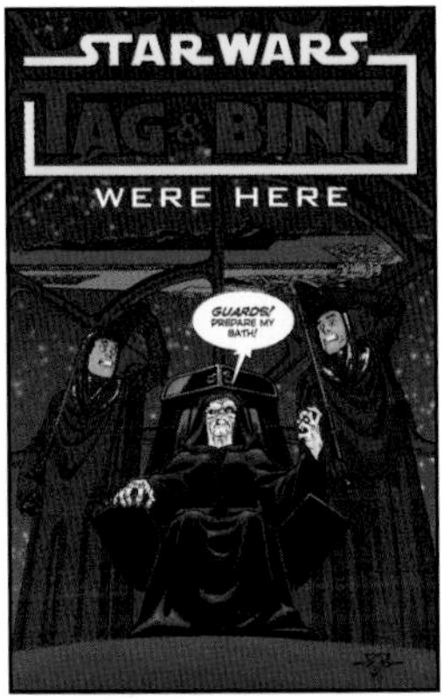
STAR WARS
TAG & BINK
WERE HERE
GUARDS! PREPARE MY BATH!

TAG AND BINK WERE HERE

Laugh yourself into orbit with the hilarious misadventures of a pair of hapless Rebel officers!

ISBN 978-1-59307-641-2 | $14.99

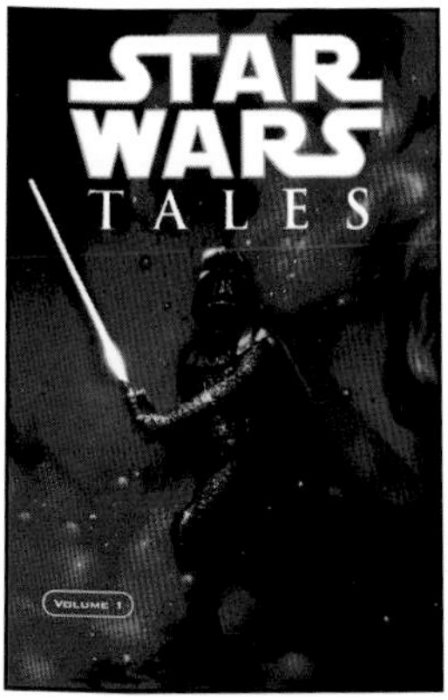
STAR WARS
TALES
VOLUME 1

TALES VOLUME 1

Collecting the first four issues of the successful quarterly anthology, this exciting volume explores every corner of the *Star Wars* galaxy!

ISBN 978-1-56971-619-9 | $19.99

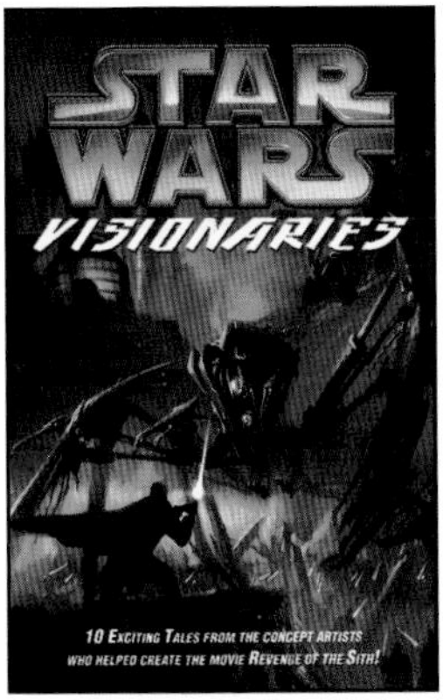
STAR WARS
VISIONARIES
10 EXCITING TALES FROM THE CONCEPT ARTISTS WHO HELPED CREATE THE MOVIE REVENGE OF THE SITH!

VISIONARIES

Ten exciting tales from the concept artists who helped create the movie *Revenge of the Sith*!

ISBN 978-1-59307-311-4 | $17.99

DARK HORSE BOOKS

AVAILABLE AT YOUR LOCAL COMICS SHOP OR BOOKSTORE!

To find a comics shop in your area, call 1-888-266-4226

For more information or to order direct, visit darkhorse.com or call 1-800-862-0052 Mon.–Fri. 9 AM to 5 PM Pacific Time.

Prices and availability subject to change without notice.

STAR WARS®
CLONE WARS ADVENTURES

Don't miss any of the action-packed adventures of your favorite **STAR WARS®** characters, available at comics shops and bookstores in a galaxy near you!

$6.95 each!

Volume 1	**Volume 2**	**Volume 3**	**Volume 4**	**Volume 5**
ISBN 978-1-59307-243-8	ISBN 978-1-59307-271-1	ISBN 978-1-59307-307-7	ISBN 978-1-59307-402-9	ISBN 978-1-59307-483-8
Volume 6	**Volume 7**	**Volume 8**	**Volume 9**	**Volume 10**
ISBN 978-1-59307-567-5	ISBN 978-1-59307-678-8	ISBN 978-1-59307-680-1	ISBN 978-1-59307-832-4	ISBN 978-1-59307-878-2